Faculty-Administration
Relationships

Faculty-Administration

Relationships

REPORT OF A WORK CONFERENCE

MAY 7-9, 1957, *SPONSORED BY THE*
COMMISSION ON INSTRUCTION AND
EVALUATION OF THE AMERICAN
COUNCIL ON EDUCATION

EDITED BY FRANK C. ABBOTT

AMERICAN COUNCIL ON EDUCATION
Washington, D.C.

PRINTED IN THE UNITED STATES OF AMERICA

Foreword

THE COMMISSION ON INSTRUCTION AND EVALUATION HAS BEEN INTERested in a number of matters that are of concern equally to teachers and administrators, such as questions of curriculum, of the deployment of faculty time among teaching, research, and service, and of appraisal of over-all institutional performance. In the course of debate on some of these issues, it recognized that, whatever one's definition of the right relation between teachers and administrators, the state of relationships was not invariably all that it might be. At the suggestion of one of its members, Dean Harold W. Stoke, then of the University of Washington and later of New York University, the commission began a series of discussions of the sources of misunderstanding and conflict between faculties and administrators. The meeting that is reported here was the culmination of these discussions.

The commission and the Council are indebted to the distinguished leaders who joined with the commission members in this inquiry, and especially to those guests who presented their own analyses, either of the sources of tensions or of relevant experience and insight in some of the fields of academic inquiry that might contribute to the resolution of undesirable conflict on the college campus. They are indebted also to the Carnegie Corporation, whose grant to the Council in support of small conferences and other selected activities, made this report possible.

ARTHUR S. ADAMS, *President*
American Council on Education

June 3, 1958

v

Preface

UNIVERSITIES AND COLLEGES PRESENT SPECIAL PROBLEMS FOR THE STU-
dent of organization and administration to analyze and, one hopes,
to understand. For one thing they pose objectives that are less tangible and less subject to "quality control" than, say, the making of tin
cans at a profit. One may be able to judge how sound a given educational experience has been; but it is risky to draw a line as of any
one time and say that the outcomes of a given course of study have
been such and so. Further, the essential "fabricating machines" of
universities are human beings, just as are the raw materials; there
is no more intensely human organization than the college or university. The circumstances of academic organization do not rule out
the needfulness and usefulness of determining administrative principle, but they make principle much harder to discover and to interpret in the light of the rich variety of individual human qualities
and situations.

In spite of—perhaps because of—the complexity of establishing
principles of academic organization and administration, there has
been little research on many aspects of college and university administration. Indeed, as a search of literature rapidly shows, there
has even been little thoughtful or systemic discussion of fundamental administrative problems.

The Commission on Instruction and Evaluation of the American
Council on Education is interested in the relations of teachers and
administrators because it is clear that, wherever the principles may
lie, these are the forces which, together with the students, determine the quality and effectiveness of higher education programs.
The commission interested itself in faculty-administration relationships without reaching prior conclusions as to what the desirable
status of these relationships might be. It has rightly been said that
"happiness" is not, in colleges, a criterion of success; the "happiest"
department on the campus may be *either* the strongest or the least
imaginative and productive. It may well be true that a certain ten-

vi

sion between faculty and administration is evidence of sound academic health.

But if it is true that there is an essential virtue in an opposition of views where objectives are intangible and where performance in many ways defies measurement, it is also true that there can be no constructive outcome of an opposition that degenerates into petty bickering for personal or departmental advantage, where motives are usually suspect or misunderstood, where communication breaks down among those who have no obligation to agree but who do have an obligation always to seek better answers. The commission has spent much time pondering the problems of curriculum, instruction, and evaluation in the face of rapidly expanding enrollments and a constricting supply of well-prepared teachers, and has been concerned that in some places the relationships between faculties and administrators may impede the efforts of institutions to deal with these problems effectively.

The meeting that is reported here was arranged with the idea that many specialized fields have contributions to make to the analysis and understanding of academic administration. The publication is evidence, not of a conclusion by the conference or by the commission that final answers have been found, but rather of the thought that some of the basic questions should be of wider interest.

The commission hopes that these papers and excerpts from the discussion will stimulate debate and inquiry among teachers and administrators in many disciplines and on many campuses as to the "right relation" of the forces of higher education on the campus. It will welcome comments and proposals based upon this report and upon the debate that it hopes the report will stimulate. Out of widespread debate and study should come increased understanding of the differing functions and responsibilities of the various agencies that are essential parties to the effective academic program.

ELMER ELLIS, *Chairman,*
Commission on Instruction and Evaluation

March 31, 1958

Conference Roster

MEMBERS OF THE COMMISSION ON INSTRUCTION AND EVALUATION

Appointed by the American Council on Education

Elmer Ellis, President, University of Missouri; *Chairman*

Omer Clyde Aderhold, President, University of Georgia

Leonard Beach, Dean, Graduate School, Vanderbilt University

William C. Fels, Associate Provost, Columbia University; subsequently President, Bennington College

C. C. Fries,[1] Professor of English, University of Michigan

Thomas H. Hamilton, Vice-President for Academic Affairs, Michigan State University

Rev. Theodore M. Hesburgh, C.S.C., President, University of Notre Dame

Nancy Duke Lewis, Dean of Pembroke College, Brown University

T. R. McConnell, Professor of Education, University of California, Berkeley

Phebe Ward, Principal, Galileo Adult School, San Francisco

Martin D. Whitaker, President, Lehigh University

Frank C. Abbott, Staff Associate, American Council on Education; *Secretary to the Commission*

OTHER CONFERENCE PARTICIPANTS

Alan K. Campbell, Associate Professor of Political Science, Hofstra College

Ralph N. Campbell, Professor of Industrial and Labor Relations, Cornell University

[1] Professor Fries was out of the country at the time of the conference.

Ralph F. Fuchs, General Secretary, American Association of University Professors; on leave as Professor of Law, Indiana University

Charles Garside, President, Associated Hospital Service of New York; Trustee, State University of New York

H. J. Heneman, Partner, Cresap, McCormick and Paget

Frederick H. Jackson, Executive Assistant, Carnegie Corporation of New York

Loren C. Petry, Professor of Botany, Emeritus, Cornell University

Richard H. Sullivan, President, Reed College

Ralph W. Tyler, Director, Center for Advanced Study in the Behavioral Sciences

York Willbern, Professor of Political Science; Director, Bureau of Public Administration, University of Alabama

Logan Wilson, President, University of Texas

W. Max Wise, Professor of Education, Teachers College, Columbia University

Contents

Nature and Sources of Faculty-Administration Tensions

1. *A President's Perspective*

LOGAN WILSON

PRESIDENT, UNIVERSITY OF TEXAS

A COLLEGE OR UNIVERSITY IS IN THEORY AN INTELLECTUAL COMMUNITY in which conflict and tension are at a minimum. The actual state of affairs, however, is usually somewhat different. During my firsthand experience in a dozen or more institutions of higher education, I have encountered only one situation which approximates the ideal type, and this particular organization is neither a college nor a university. It is the Center for Advanced Study in the Behavioral Sciences, near Stanford, California. As you know, the Center was established by the Ford Foundation so that a hand-picked group of forty to fifty outstanding behavioral scientists could get away each year from the impediments to higher learning which often beset scholars and scientists in even our best colleges and universities. During my visits as a board member at the Center, I have concluded from comments of fellows that the experiment is proving to be highly successful. It seems to be more conducive to productive scholarship and individual satisfactions than the environments in which the fellows normally function.

One thing they like most about the Center is the virtually unstructured situation. Administration, insofar as it affects them in any way except to find solutions for the minor problems they bring to it, is at a minimum. There are no departments, no classes to be met, no committee assignments, no scheduled activities in which anybody is required to participate. The Center gives each fellow a stipend to match his regular salary and provides him with an office, library facilities, and some research assistance. The participants all feel that they are helping to accomplish the main purpose of the Center by contributing more to the development of behavioral science than

1

they could in their usual settings. Although I had reservations about the idea prior to membership on the board, I must say that I have never observed another situation in which a group of individuals was equally productive and happy in what they are doing.

The Center has characteristics which may help explain the absence of tension. The fellows have only one responsibility, instead of several. No one formally judges or ranks their performance in any way. Their status—and that of their families—in and about the Center is relatively unimportant because it is temporary. The administration of the Center has almost no major role in keeping outsiders satisfied with the performance of the Center. The whole operation is on such a limited scale that bureaucratic administration is almost altogether unnecessary.

An unanswered question I have about the value of the Center experience is the extent to which the fellows may find difficulty in readjusting themselves to their college and university environments. Some of them may feel impelled to reshape their situations in accordance with a new focus of expectations, and perhaps this is desirable, but in most institutions it is obviously not possible. Despite the credo of academic freedom and the fact that professors enjoy a greater amount of occupational latitude than do the employees of other organizations, institutions of higher education necessarily must have definitely established and enforced lines of authority and responsibility. This being so, it is inevitable that conflicts should arise.

How does conflict manifest itself? Insofar as faculty-administration relations are concerned, it ranges from mild expressions of annoyance, dissatisfaction, and distrust to a continual state of tension which at times may break out into the open as a pitched battle, with the faculty on one side of a dispute and the administration on the other. The absence of evidences of conflict does not mean, of course, that the two parties must see eye-to-eye on all issues and form what amounts to a mutual admiration society. Disagreements are not only to be expected in a normal situation, but also are desirable even in an idealized situation. The conflict of persons, in other words, should not be confused with the competition of ideas.

One commentator, Harold W. Stoke, has asked:

How much of all this conflict is inevitable and how much avoidable? How much is inherent in the nature of organization itself—the necessity for superiority and subordination, the division of labor, the disabilities of sheer size? How much is due to problems of personality, to ineptness, to inexperience, to faulty organization? What steps can be taken to reduce strain? In what specific fields does it most frequently arise—financial, public relations, personnel, educational philosophy and conviction? Perhaps the subject is worth more concentrated attention than it has received.

In answer to Dr. Stoke, it may be noted that whereas colleges and universities are characterized by the conjunctive social processes of accommodation and cooperation, the disjunctive processes of competition and conflict are ubiquitous. In human affairs, these latter processes occur when some persons think that other persons hinder, block, or otherwise impede the realization of their desires, and a state of tension typically results. When competition ceases to be impersonal, it shades over into conflict in activity directed toward ends not easily achieved. Thus, the clashing of interests may turn participants into adversaries, and activity may assume the form of a combat. In competition, energy or activity is largely deflected toward weakening or even eliminating the opposition. This is why, of course, actions leading to the dismissal or attempted dismissal of academic personnel, either faculty or administrative, are often the culminating events which attract the most outside attention to serious intramural conflict.

It is of no particular value to list here the familiar symptoms or evidences of conflict. Perhaps we should expect what is referred to in the Army as a "normal level of griping." Both casual observation and careful surveys confirm the impression that almost everywhere faculties are restive about low salaries, heavy teaching loads, lack of research and secretarial assistance, burdensome committee work, inadequate office space and laboratory facilities, faulty promotion policies, administrative arbitrariness or vacillation, and so on. Professors, in brief, do not differ materially from others in desiring higher pay, shorter hours, more job security, speedier promotion—and, in general, more satisfactory working conditions. Furthermore, a vague sense of frustration about these matters can be given a more satisfactory emotional focus when blame is attached to concrete entities such as administrative officers.

Although nobody seems to bother very much about whether administrators themselves are restive concerning their working conditions and faculties, they, too, have their chronic complaints. Their accountability is spread more widely than that of the faculty, however, and hence the causes of their tension are more diffuse and perhaps less likely to be rationalized in terms of faculty provocations. Like the ancient deity Janus, they must always look in different directions for hazards in the offing, but unlike him, they are endowed with neither immortality or omnipotence. Vicariously, at least, most of the frustrations of the faculty are *ipso facto* the administrator's own frustrations; also, there is the pressure of a widely held sentiment that it is his responsibility, regardless of authority or means at hand, to do something about alleviating faculty frustrations. Except for those who are incurable optimists, it is no wonder, then, that some administrators become calloused by conflict or else are reduced to a constant state of tension.

Most administrators, to be sure, recognize that they earn their pay mainly in trying to solve problems stemming from and created by other persons. Some find this exciting, others overwhelming. Here I am reminded that not long ago I inquired of an acquaintance about a certain administrative officer in his relatively new post. "Oh," he said, "haven't you heard? He got fed up with working on other people's problems and went back to teaching, where he could pick his own problems." When I related this to another person who also knew the former administrator, he added, "What he meant was that it is more fun just to be a problem."

It seems reasonable to assume that conflicts and tensions are to some extent inevitable in any large and complex social organization. Their most common manifestations may and often do take the form of minor disjunctions which neither undermine the structure nor seriously interfere with the functioning of an institution of higher learning. Academic life would be pleasanter without them; but, despite the current fetish being made of "adjustment" and "getting along," few persons would contend that the main criterion of successful functioning for a college or university should be the absence of frictions or that its main purpose should be to afford contentment to those in its employ.

Our real concern, therefore, should be with faculty-administrative disjunctions which are readily avoidable, and more especially with those which seriously impede the achievement of institutional goals. To avoid, or at least minimize, the severe kinds of conflict and tension, we must first locate their causes. These, it seems to me, necessarily must be centered in the following: attitudes and values, persons, and the structure itself.

Beginning with attitudes and values, it should be repeated that the broadly accepted ends of institutions of higher learning are to conserve, diffuse, and advance learning. Honest differences of opinion may turn into conflict, however, in the specification of this objective. Without attempting to establish any order of importance or go into any details, I shall simply list some of the more familiar issues which frequently precipitate divisive alignments.

1. Long-range objectives: Belief that a large institution, particularly a state university, has an obligation in effect to "be all things to all men," versus the view that it should confine itself to traditional aims. Regarding all aims as being of equal importance versus the opinion that realism demands an assignment of priorities. The leadership concept versus the response-to-needs concept. Diffused aims, such as "the pursuit of truth," versus adherence to clearly specified objectives. Over-all objectives versus departmental and individual ambitions. Relative emphases to be placed on teaching, research, and public service.

2. Allocation of means: By whom? Through what procedures? Criteria—need, merit, the "squeaking wheel principle," publicity values, and so on. With or without regard to outside pressures?

3. The curriculum: Liberal and general education versus vocationalism and specialization. Vested interests in the *status quo* versus recognized needs for curricular modifications. (As someone has said, changing the curriculum entails all the physical and psychological difficulties of moving a cemetery.)

4. Organization: The fetish of democracy and freedom and the tendency to proliferate rules and regulations to the point where, as Ernest O. Melby has said, freedom to act becomes hamstrung. Confusion between decisions having to do with professional authority and those relating to administrative responsibility. Overt recognition of the necessity for a division of labor versus the covert belief that everybody should try to do everybody else's washing.

5. Members of the organization: The academic tradition of a "body of equals" versus sharp disparities in individual worth to the institution. Individual desires for more certainty, security, and participation in important institutional decisions versus the dislike for red tape, inflexibility, and the distractions of "outside" concerns.

These and many other issues make it obvious that colleges and universities are usually in a state of disequilibrium about intermediate ends as well as ways and means. Although there may be a consensus regarding ultimate objectives, there is no unitary output, as there normally is in a business corporation, and no annual balance sheet in simple form against which endeavor may be objectively appraised. Stockholders are nonexistent in academic enterprise and the board of directors or regents typically leave to the faculty and administration the settlement of most disagreements of the kind mentioned. To be sure, as will be noted presently, there are usually structural mechanisms for the handling of differences and disputes over matters regarded as important, and if these are carefully thought out and well established, more light than heat will result.

Sometimes, however, the ground rules are not adequate, and even when they are, there may be faculty and administrative participants whose personalities and behavior are sources of conflict. To put it another way, there often are a certain number of problem people around whose attitudes and actions interfere with the harmonious and effective functioning of the institution.

Here the observation should be made that those persons who never cause any trouble may likewise be those who contribute very little to the on-going purposes of a college or university. Henry Wriston has noted that, "Far greater errors have resulted from timidity, indecision, and inaction than from the patently tyrannous misbehavior of a few heads of institutions." I would add also that in terms of effective institutional functioning, the real problem people on most faculties are not the obstructionists but the mediocrities. As is the case with popular and not especially competent administrators, these individuals are often very likable personalities, and this is precisely the reason nobody ever had the courage to get rid of them. Our immediate concern, however, is not with the miscellaneous shortcomings of faculty members and administrative officers, but only with those objectionable types who, as Donald C. Stone has indicated, ". . . endeavor to thwart the legitimate function of other persons and groups . . . sow dissension and controversy, and concentrate on issues which are divisive."

Because of faulty initial selection, absence of an "up or out" policy of retention, procrastination, or buck-passing in the matter of unpleasant decisions, and an obsession with the individual prerogatives rather than the institutional consequences of tenure, almost every college and university has on its faculty some persons whose actions foment conflict. The damage they can do depends on a number of factors, such as the kind and size of the institution, faculty and administrative attitudes toward their behavior, the stability of the structure, and so on. From an administrative point of view, I would classify some of the more common types of faculty deviants as follows:

1. Fundamentally disordered personalities: Any sizable enterprise is likely to have in its membership some maladjusted individuals who simply cannot function amicably and effectively in any kind of normal environment. Since a college or university chooses its professional employees largely on the basis of technical competence and often pays scant attention to personality traits, it is perhaps to be expected that there is sometimes a fairly high proportion of "screw-balls." Both the system of tenure and the respect accorded the "independent spirit" in academic circles, furthermore, result in a greater measure of tolerance for difficult persons than would be found in almost any comparable social system.

2. The frustrated and disgruntled: Every employing organization of any size and complexity will likewise have some members who place a higher value on their services than do those who must evaluate them. Frustration in turn may lead to disgruntled attitudes and behavior toward those who exercise these judgments. Human nature being what it is, there is a tendency to place the blame on flaws in the structure and on shortcomings of those most directly responsible for it—administrators. Whatever energies may initially have been channeled into teaching and research often become heavily diverted into schemes of protest and other efforts to redefine the situation more to the disgruntled individual's liking. In short, by his own consistently antagonistic activities, the faculty person in question comes

to be known to the administration and to many of his colleagues as a "sorehead" or troublemaker.

3. The misfits: Faculty misfits may be defined as those who insist on playing roles other than the ones in which they are cast as teachers, scholars, or scientists. They are typically less interested in the pursuit of truth than in missionary activity, partisanship, and the promotion of various causes. Frequently combining emotional fervor with a tendency toward exhibitionism, they regard the classroom and the faculty meeting less as places to solve problems and examine different points of view than as sounding boards for a particular gospel. Regardless of the sincerity of their motives, the net effect of their actions is often to involve the institution in controversies which seriously impede its support and forward movement. Sometimes, of course, as one commentator has put it, they are really carrying batons under their coats and are waiting hopefully to assume direction of the organization itself.

Although some of the deviant types enclaved in the ranks of the faculty would get short shrift in administrative roles, these latter posts also produce their own special varieties of miscreants. Indeed, I think it can be fairly said that whenever a serious conflict rends a college or university, the administration is necessarily more at fault than any person or group of persons on the faculty. My reason for this assertion is that one of the primary obligations of top administration is to prevent conflict, and, hence, any continuing and deep conflict is prima-facie evidence of administrative ineptness. My point is, not that the administration should yield to the faculty in a dispute over principles or other matters, but merely that it is the duty of administration to keep impasses from developing.

In view of the extremely diffuse responsibilities of most key positions in academic administration, the persons who occupy them are ordinarily chosen with at least as much of an eye to their personal characteristics as to their technical qualifications. Furthermore, diverse individuals and groups normally participate in the selection process. For these reasons, administrative posts are seldom occupied by near-psychotics, misanthropes, soreheads, and other types who are prone by disposition to be troublemakers. One of the difficulties in picking the right person for key administrative posts, however, is that the inexperienced appointee always involves a situational risk.

Professors presumably acquire tenure only after they have demonstrated their worth in the lower ranks by performance at essentially the same kind of tasks. Deans and presidents, on the other hand, are often lifted from virtually unrelated assignments into totally new and different responsibilities.

None is ever drafted against his will, to be sure, and most have supposedly demonstrated some aptitude for educational leadership. But few people, including those who name administrators, realize that to move from a professorship to a presidency is to change occupation, as someone has aptly said. It is therefore inevitable that some errors should be made, and a mistake on this level is by definition a serious mistake. The appointee may discover what he thought was a leadership role is in large part a sort of brokerage function, or that he cannot avoid spending a good part of his time acting merely as a shock absorber or buffer.

Subjected as he may be to pressures from all directions and often from opposite directions, the administrative officer may readily fail to develop as a real leader or may deteriorate into a "buck-passer," or weaseler. In so doing he inadvertently gives rise to situations where conflict and tension may become rife. This same thing holds when he conceives of himself primarily as an officeholder who performs ritualistic and routine functions. At the other extreme is the martinet or authoritarian who conceives his job as that of running the institution in the same way that the owner of a small business may operate when he is the entire management and everybody else is merely a salaried or wage-earning employee. Although the "boss" is a vanishing phenomenon in all forms of corporate enterprise today, he still persists strongly enough as a mental image to cause faculties to keep him in mind in drawing up their codes of ethics and articles of government. Properly sensitized administrators, accordingly, need always to consult with the faculty if they are to avoid giving credence to the widely held belief that they and their kind are motivated by a "Jehovah complex" in "doing God's will."

Even with the right attitudes or values and with capable persons in the faculty and administration to carry them out, an institution may still flounder for want of proper social organization. Although there is admittedly no one form of organization equally well suited to all educational needs, it is surprising to observe how many existing structures fall short of meeting basic requirements for smooth and effective functioning. Some of the more prevalent shortcomings might be classified as follows:

1. Gaps between responsibility and authority: One difficulty of the typical college or university as a form of social organization is that certain responsibilities may be diffused throughout the entire system to the extent that accountability gets lost. Correspondingly, authority to see that particular tasks get performed may turn into a kind of academic shell game. As Robert Hutchins has pointed out, an institution has to decide "whether it wishes to be managed by an administrator or ornamented by an officeholder."

Reluctant to make "hard" (unpopular but necessary) decisions themselves, faculty committees, departmental chairmen, and deans may pass matters of this sort up to the president's office. Desiring to avoid being unpopular himself, the president sometimes passes such matters down the line or else tries to formulate blanket rules and regulations to avoid the exercise of individual discretion. In contrast to Army procedure, there is nobody on the academic scene who issues orders and then sees that they are carried out. If one were seeking an analogy to academic processes of government in some colleges and universities, perhaps the nearest thing would be a perpetual debating society. Such goings-on are enjoyed thoroughly by academic "windbags" and parliamentarians, of course, but they are extremely frustrating to the majority who would prefer to move ahead with the real business of higher education.

2. Ambiguities in the division of labor: Many academicians strongly feel that everybody on the faculty is entitled to have a hand in all important policy matters, so that there is a sentiment favoring committee management, innumerable group meetings, and other time-consuming procedures on the grounds that they are democratic. One difficulty with this mode of organization is that faculty representatives are accustomed to thinking in terms of departmental and other specialized interests, whereas many of the problems to be solved require an institution-wide perspective.

Furthermore, as someone has noted, there are structural requirements of efficient bureaucratic organization which probably set sharp limits to the amount of feasible decentralization and spreading of control. Regardless of ritual and precedent, inherent conservatism and inertia, there is on occasion a need to get things done promptly, so that some centralized authority has to override the vested interests of particular individuals and compartmentalized groups. Confusion is compounded by the fact that many faculty members are administrative officers, and vice versa, and by the fact that lines cannot be clearly drawn always between what is or is not properly a matter for administrative action. Such ambiguities and uncertainties necessarily result in varying amounts of tension among participants as well as nonparticipants.

3. Categorization of members: Even though academicians are professional men and women enjoying a high degree of independence as specialists, they function within an institutional framework which evaluates, ranks, and rewards them in terms of their presumed value to the organization. The whole process is so complex that it is inevitably a source of misunderstanding, and the results are unavoidably a further source of real or alleged grievance to some individuals. All of this runs counter to the body-of-equals tradition, but apparently there is no organizational substitute for it, not only as an incentive device, but also as a means for ordering the allocation of limited ends. In contrasting the flat and hierarchical patterns, there is some experimental evidence to indicate that in the former variety, members of the organization may be happier but less efficient whereas in the latter they will be more efficient but not as happy. In any event, this structural aspect of the college or university seems to be a source of considerable tension and conflict.

4. Faulty communication mechanisms: Many faculty-administrative conflicts have their origin in misinformation, partial information, or lack of information on both sides. Thus, the manner in which a decision is reached or an action accomplished is often of critical importance in gaining full acceptance and implementation. And certainly this is one area in which improvement can be made.

In conclusion, I want to issue a reminder that my focus on the problems of faculty-administrative relations has necessarily emphasized disjunctive rather than conjunctive processes and weak rather than strong points. The longevity of most colleges and universities is prima-facie evidence of their successful functioning as social organizations. Even though our colleges and universities exhibit many shortcomings and imperfections, it is my observation that most persons who have chosen the academic profession regard their environment as the one they prefer to all others. However this may be, we should acknowledge that the college or university as a form of social organization has not been subjected to the same intensive analysis and study which have been brought to bear on various forms of business and industrial enterprise in an effort to improve the morale and working efficiency of employees.

I would, therefore, end on the positive note that we all need to address ourselves more objectively to these aspects of what we are doing and try to devise ways of further improving our institutions of higher learning.

2. A Faculty View

LOREN C. PETRY
PROFESSOR OF BOTANY, EMERITUS, CORNELL UNIVERSITY

IT IS CUSTOMARY TO DEFINE THE FUNCTION OF THE COLLEGE OR UNIVERSITY as the conservation, diffusion, and augmentation of knowledge. The effect of its efforts, particularly on the students but also on the public at large, is commonly called education. The personnel of the college or university consists of four groups: clerical and other employees, of no relevance to this discussion; students and alumni; faculty; and administration. As everywhere else in human affairs, tensions exist in colleges and universities between individuals and between groups. The tensions between groups within it sometimes contribute to the effectiveness of the operations of the college or university, sometimes detract. Tensions between faculty and administration, when mild, are usually considered to be beneficial, but detrimental if they are violent or long continued. Detrimental tensions are commonly resolved by *ad hoc* measures or by time, less often by the use of measures based on a systematic analysis of their nature and sources. We are here engaged in an attempt to make such an analysis, and I am specifically directed to speak from the point of view of the faculty.

Since education is the prime concern of the faculty, one of its aspects requires comment. In essence education is a process of inducing controlled changes in human behavior. Experience shows that this process is difficult, slow, and capable of only limited acceleration. Instruction may be accomplished by mass-production techniques, education cannot. And unless the history of man's development is a wholly false guide, the improvement of educational method by some revolutionary breakthrough of technique is as improbable as the sudden development of some new method of human reproduction. We are, in short, dealing with an aspect of human activity in which a rapid increase in productivity to match rapid increase in cost cannot be hoped for. This needs special emphasis at this time when both business and industry are, at least in part, in that happy position. This real but unwelcome limitation on the amount of educational result that a faculty may be expected to produce is a frequently unrecognized source of tension between faculty and administration.

Since the Second World War the administrative machinery of colleges and universities has been enlarged to enable it to deal with problems created by increased numbers of students and by other factors. This enlargement has been largely accomplished by the introduction of new officers—vice-presidents and the like—to occupy positions between the top administrative officers and the faculty. In most institutions this phase of rapid enlargement of the administrative machinery has been completed. Some of the most serious sources of tension between faculty and administration lie in this administrative structure and in the qualifications of the personnel selected to fill its posts. Only a part of this tension is caused by the recent changes in administrative structure, but these changes have served to direct faculty attention to the nature of administrative organization and procedure.

1. Students and alumni: The students, undergraduate and graduate, and the alumni are of some importance as a source of tension between faculty and administration. The graduate students frequently serve as faculty members in part, and they have the general characteristics of the faculty and share its point of view. In general, tensions between faculty and administration produced by the students are sporadic in their occurrence, special in character to the

point of defying classification, and, on the whole, of relatively minor importance. They are accordingly dismissed from further discussion here. Special interests of the alumni, such as athletics, admissions policy, and the like, sometimes produce serious tensions. But these also constitute special problems and are omitted here.

2. Faculty: In spite of a general opinion to the contrary, the faculty, including all ranks, is remarkably homogeneous in character. All faculty members come largely from the same general social background. They have all had much the same training and experience. They are individualists; that is, they are nonconformists, in small matters at least, and frequently in larger ones. They are ambitious, dissatisfied, critical, and committed to education as a career.

3. Administration: The administration of the American college or university consists of three distinct groups of persons, and these groups require careful characterization.

a) Academic administration: This group consists of those administrative officers who are partly or entirely concerned with academic matters. Deans, provosts, vice-presidents, and presidents are typical members of the group. They are recruited almost entirely from faculties and accordingly have much the same personal characteristics as faculty members. They occasionally are able to continue with part-time instruction, but almost never with scientific research or scholarly publication.

b) Nonacademic administration: Administrative officers concerned largely or entirely with nonacademic matters make up this group. The superintendent of buildings and grounds, the treasurer, the registrar, the dean of students—these members of the group have been with us for a long time. The vice-president for development, the public relations counselor, the alumni secretary as an appointee of the institution, rather than of the alumni—these are more recent arrivals. These newcomers to the group are specialists in their fields and they have been recruited from practitioners in those fields. They have been journalists, businessmen, lawyers, and the like, but rarely have they been faculty members.

c) Governing boards: The wide variety of boards of trustees, regents, overseers, managers, and so on, is too well known to require description here. These are, in general, policy-making bodies that delegate to administrative officers the work of carrying out these policies. They occasionally perform detailed administrative work, but not often. Such boards have several characteristics that should be noted. They hold title to the property of the institution, and have full legal authority to manage the institution. They seldom have a membership of less than five, and may consist of forty or more members. And their membership usually includes few or no faculty members, either of the institution concerned or of any other, either active or retired.

In our effort to locate the sources of tensions between faculty and administration it is pertinent to compare the faculty with these administrative groups with regard to three factors: background, training, and interests; personal characteristics; and responsibilities.

When we compare faculty members with academic administrators, it is clear that in general they have identical backgrounds, training, and interests. Deans are sometimes chosen from business or industry, and presidents may have been lawyers or ministers; but such cases are relatively rare. There are some significant differences in personal characteristics. For one of these, hear Sir Charles Snow (better known as C. P. Snow), Civil Service Commissioner for Great Britain since 1945, in *The Listener*, April 18, 1957. Speaking of managers, he says, "What are they like? The answer is, much like you and me. But I believe there are some respects in which, on the average, the managers of the world are significantly a little different from you and me. To begin with, they like managing. They like responsibility—that is what the managers say. They like power—that is what the managed say."

The significant difference between faculty and academic administration is of course in the nature of their responsibilities. The professor must educate; the academic administrator must keep the academic machine running, must meet deadlines, above all must make decisions, many of which vitally affect the faculty. This difference in responsibility, especially if complicated by failure of communication and a little ineptitude, can be a prolific source of tension.

A similar comparison of faculty and nonacademic administration shows that these two groups have substantially nothing in common but adjacent working quarters and places on a common payroll. The faculty and governing boards do not have even these in common;

their only common interest is in the institution and a loyalty to what it may stand for. That this diversity is a source of tension can be shown. Whether it provides a countervailing source of strength is outside the scope of this discussion.

This is in outline the organization within which arise the tensions we are concerned with. At least three sources of such tensions can be readily identified and illustrated. These sources are: the increased complexity of the administrative machinery itself; the training, experience, and personal characteristics of nonacademic administrators; and policy decisions affecting faculty. The following situations, unfortunately not rare, will serve to illustrate these, in the order stated.

1. Increased complexity of administrative machinery: New administrative positions are usually created for either or both of two purposes—to divide a load of work or to take over new functions that have become important. The new administrator will need information to guide him in the making of decisions, and much of this information must be obtained from the faculty. As the new office develops, the paper work not related to education grows. This may be only a grievance, but the cumulative effect is tension.

Under the best of conditions the communication between faculty and administration is seldom adequate. As the machinery becomes more complex, the system of communication, however carefully devised and faithfully employed, begins to fail. A considerable failure of real communication between faculty and administration can be found in most cases of strong tension.

The introduction of vice-presidents, provosts, and other officers to whom the president delegates some of his duties has produced a special irritation. The new officer is more accessible than the president and, to the extent he has power, he expedites business effectively. In too many cases, however, he has been given veto power only, and affirmative decisions can only be made by the president as before. If in addition the vice-president's veto is final, or if an appeal is frowned upon, a serious situation can result. In all these cases a change in either policy or structure will reduce the tension.

2. Activities of nonacademic administrators: Decisions affecting the educational work of an institution should be made by persons competent in that work—that is, by faculty members and academic

administrators. It occasionally happens that a registrar, given duties of scheduling, begins to modify class schedules or to set examination dates arbitrarily. The faculty reaction is usually prompt, but a residue of tension remains. Plant maintenance men or purchasing agents, schooled to prevent waste, can hamper the educational work of an institution by delaying needed repairs or installations or by haggling over purchases in an effort to save money. This is correct procedure from their point of view, but the faculty view is that the purpose of the institution is to educate, cheaply if possible, but to educate.

The most serious tensions in this area are produced by public relations men and fund-raising officers who make public statements that seem to present an inaccurate picture of the institution and its work. In efforts to influence public opinion or prospective donors they sometimes seem to commit the institution to activities so distinct from education that we might suppose the colleges and universities are following the lead of business and industry and are planning to "diversify." These situations are especially difficult because there is no recognized procedure for the faculty to follow in making its protest against the accidental or calculated indiscretion of a high officer of the institution. To remove such sources of tension a change in administrative personnel is indicated.

3. Lack of frankness on the part of administrative officers: The most usual form of this is the suppression of information about matters of faculty concern under administrative consideration until it is too late for the opinion of the faculty to be brought to bear on them. There are matters in which the faculty has an important interest and which should be initially explored in private. There are other conditions under which public discussion should be invited from the start. If full information about college and university business is freely given to the faculty, unless there are compelling reasons against this course of action, tensions in many institutions will be notably reduced.

4. Effects of the low economic status of the faculty: The facts about the economic status of the faculty are well known, but some of its effects deserve attention because of their impact on faculty morale.

a) To recruit staff, new appointments are being regularly made at or above the salaries of older, more experienced, and more competent men.

b) The wives of young faculty members find it necessary to hold jobs to make ends meet, and so the family is delayed, sometimes well toward middle life.

c) A faculty member in the middle of a successful career finds it difficult or impossible to send his children to the college of his or their choice because of expense.

d) As a faculty member approaches retirement, he finds that the retirement allowance that seemed (and was) adequate when it was being earned is now far from adequate.

These and similar considerations cause an increase in tension as each annual budget is being prepared. Under these conditions, it is not surprising that there is faculty dissatisfaction when the chairman of a governing board explains that money from general funds is being appropriated for a new building now, rather than later, because building costs are rising!

These examples show some of the immediate causes of tension between faculty and administration. However, they are symptomatic only; the real source is deeper. For clues to this, the talk in faculty clubs is a better guide than the titles of papers read at educational meetings. Occurrences such as the following give us indications of the nature of that source.

A governing board, confronted with an important difference of opinion between the president and the faculty, instead of investigating and possibly mediating, follows the practice of business and either supports the president fully or asks for his resignation.

Educational problems common to the institutions of a state or other limited area are studied, not by committees made up of appropriate members of their faculties, but by the presidents of the institutions. Practical solutions are required, it is explained. Since "practical solutions" are usually compromises, the presidents begin with compromises, basic principles are not examined, and only compromise solutions are ever arrived at.

A governing board, accustomed to the methods of business and industry, and with the confidence that power confers, decides questions of the greatest importance to an educational institution on the recommendation of its own committee which may have had the advice and counsel of a single educator, the president of the institution.

George Pope Shannon devoted a well-spent page of the Spring 1957 number of the *AAUP Bulletin* to another example. Hear Mr. Shannon:

A recent editorial in a publication devoted to problems of educational administration takes note of imminent "pressures" (e.g., an 85% increase in enrollment by 1970; "the multiplying educational needs and demands of American Society") that will compel "rationalization of college and university structure and process." The editorial hails this coming "rationalization" as "a high adventure in professional self-appraisal by educators who may be expected to apply their customary objectivity and scientific search for evidence" to problems of "the adequacy of the curriculum, teaching methods, administrative process and structure, and financial management of institutions." As the outcome of these adventures, "a comprehensive and comparable picture of patterns of American higher education should begin to emerge."

Needless to say, the teaching members of the academic profession have a considerable interest in any emerging "picture of patterns" for higher education. Unfortunately, it is probable that these teaching members will not be found in great numbers among those called upon to engage in this high adventure. The adventurers will be college and university officers and trustees, and representatives of their organizations, with a scattering of "name" laymen. It is to them that the grants are going; they man the programs at the meetings of the great national associations (ours excepted) dealing with higher education; they composed the President's Commission on Higher Education in 1946; and they are members of the present President's Committee on Education Beyond the High School.

Situations such as these are hard to interpret fairly. They seem to indicate lack of confidence on the part of high administrators and governing boards in the competence of faculty members in practical affairs. It is probable that the general abilities of faculty members are more highly regarded in their communities and by the public at large than by the higher administrative officers of their institutions. Consider, in a very practical and complicated matter, the support given to Vannevar Bush, Enrico Fermi, the Comptons, and the rest—all professors at one time or another. And note that in *Who's Who in America* the economic adviser to the President of the United States describes himself as a "university professor."

The reason that the higher administrators of colleges and universities show no interest in faculty participation in decision-making

at the higher level is not, I suggest, that they doubt faculty competence; there is a very different reason. I submit that the members of
governing boards are not accustomed to the participation of their
subordinates in decision-making at the highest level and see nothing
to be gained by introducing the practice here; that they are accustomed to dealing with matters in which it is easier to arrive at a
demonstrably correct answer than it is in the field of education; that
they feel themselves fully informed when they have been briefed by
the president or other officer or by a committee; and that it has
never occurred to them that, even when fully informed, they may
still not be competent to deal with such matters.

Put in other words, I suggest that these situations result from the
training, experience, and personal characteristics of the members of
the governing boards of American colleges and universities; that our
colleges and universities are being managed by amateurs—gifted
amateurs, in many cases, it may be—but still amateurs.

The value of these governing boards in furnishing to the institutions absolutely essential financial and political support and, for the
most part, wise direction and control, cannot be questioned. But so
long as governing boards are constituted as at present, a fundamental source of tension between faculty and administration will exist.
Speculation about remedies, even the obvious one, is outside the
scope of this inquiry.

Comments

1. RALPH FUCHS
GENERAL SECRETARY, AMERICAN ASSOCIATION
OF UNIVERSITY PROFESSORS

I AM VERY GLAD TO SAY THAT FROM MY VANTAGE POINT I FEEL IM-
pelled, first, to agree with President Wilson that we are not dealing
with a situation which is fundamentally bad. I think academic institutions in this country do not have to make apologies for the over-all
degree of the success with which they operate, and that is true in
relation to the subject of our discussion this morning as well as in
relation to other matters.

The second point that has struck me about this is the enormous variety in the situations presented, especially when you take into account the many hundreds of small colleges and teachers colleges along with the great universities and the colleges which have long-established reputations.

The causal factors that produce difficulty in the small colleges are, I suppose, to a considerable degree personal. There are a good many administrators who have not come up through academic ranks. They haven't been chosen, perhaps, with the care that has been exercised in the larger institutions, and so there undoubtedly are small colleges where you have essentially a tyranny of the kind President Wilson mentioned, in which the president runs the institution more or less as though it were his own private business. Of course, where that situation prevails, you have tremendous unhappiness and essentially a bad state of affairs. My association gets asked from time to time to come and see what can be done. Well, we are not in a position to take on an inquiry into a general state of affairs in an institution if it doesn't eventuate in a violation of freedom or tenure.

Some of those complaints are doubtless unjustified; but I am quite sure that there are a good many small institutions where conditions are fundamentally unsound. I do not think this is characteristic of colleges and universities in general.

Among the three causes that President Wilson mentioned—attitudes and values, as I understood him to say, personal characteristics, and the administrative structure of academic institutions—I agree with Professor Petry it is the administrative structure that needs most of our attention. We are bound to have a variety of attitudes and values, and we are bound to have a variety of people, including some pretty obnoxious people, on faculties and sometimes in administrative posts—this is a problem to be worked on. But it is much harder to arrive at ideas for solving such a problem than it is to deal with the problems of administrative structure; and I think our main concern has to be to try to work out administrative structures and administrative methods that will somehow produce satisfactory functioning and diminish the strains, even in the face of conflicting values and the variety of people involved.

It is worth noting, too, that variety ought to continue to be greater in the academic world than in the business world and perhaps elsewhere. The very essence of the academic or educational process is to draw on variety and produce valuable results from drawing on it. In business there is complaint about the "organization man," or "yes man"; and this is a matter we in the academic world don't want to have to worry about.

Coming down to the structural factor, it seems to me that it is worth recognizing that strains are inherent wherever one person exercises authority over another. I have been interested to observe this phenomenon from the position of being the boss, so to speak, which I have occupied in the last two years for the first time in my experience in the academic world. We have a small professional staff of five members with ideal personal relationships and operate as a team to a considerable extent. But formal authority is vested in me as head of this little organization; and I find that when I get into a staff meeting and start taking up some plans and problems, I am in a different relationship to the others from the one I otherwise occupy. There do arise certain constraints, even among good friends, when the person who possesses authority is talking with those who are under him. It is hard to get a frank interchange. I feel a certain reserve at times; and when that is broken through, there may occasionally be a somewhat more acid response to something I put forth than seems to me necessary!

The difficulty in such a situation is multiplied manyfold as the organization grows in size when, as Professor Petry put it, you have filters between the top person and the people in the rank and file. The people in the rank and file may then begin to develop certain stereotypes; and the administrator who functions through filters in relation to the rank and file probably gets peculiar notions about its members, because he sees them rarely and his main personal contacts are with others, often on the outside of the institution. I suspect he often has great difficulty in really knowing his faculty.

I do not pretend to know the remedies; but they are what we are here to talk about. I want to make just one important suggestion, in accord with our democratic ideology, or obsession, as I believe President Wilson called it; and that is that there be increased delegation of authority, extending democratic processes within our institutions.

One must recognize that when delegations are made to the faculty, strains may arise from a reversal of roles. I think this has happened in relation to curricula. I have observed some administrators who, in my opinion, had sound ideas about curricula, completely frustrated and driven almost to desperation by the obstruction of a faculty majority that was proceeding without an adequate sense of responsibility and trying largely to protect the vested interests in existing courses. Hence, I do not advance delegation to the faculties as by any means a cure-all. Insofar, however, as the faculty becomes responsible for operating an institution, the strain that comes from having an authoritarian setup is reduced. Probably our principal problem is to work out the areas in which there should be delegation to the faculty and the methods whereby such delegation can be made to yield satisfactory performance. It has been done in some institutions. Curricula have been well handled by responsible faculties, although, no doubt, the methods of committee consideration have often been cumbersome and time-consuming.

There are places, of course, where the process of delegation has probably gone too far; and in some cases it hasn't been well followed up by administration or by devices that enable the faculty to function without too much committee work. Hence, it has cut too deeply into teaching and research. There are no easy answers; but we need to strive for the answers.

One thing that has to be guarded against like sin (and in a sense it is a sin) is the administrator's going ahead and doing something on his own responsibility after there has been an ostensible delegation to the faculty. I suppose that happens only occasionally; but when it happens, according to my observation, it usually happens in very critical situations. And it may happen because of what—I again agree with Professor Petry—is a key factor: namely, outside pressures, which are transmitted to the institution by administrators who are usually not in the main line. Public relations considerations are, in my view, the most serious existing obstacles to satisfactory internal functioning of colleges and universities. Time after time in critically important matters, academic administrations have simply gone ahead and acted without consultation, to the very great damage of their relations with their faculties.

This problem transcended a particular institution in a recent situation involving the 1953 statement of the Association of American Universities on the rights and responsibilities—or words to that effect—of college and university faculties. The statement came forth, and was taken by the public, as an announcement of the considered policy of the most well-known universities in the country. But the faculties had no role in formulating it, at least in some of these institutions. I think the damage to relations between administrations and faculties as a result of the statement was, just for this reason, very great indeed. The matters covered, including academic freedom, are of vital interest to the faculties and should not have been treated without faculty participation.

I think the same is true of the way athletics are handled. Athletic policy in most institutions is, I suppose, an administrative policy, although in some the faculty have full responsibility. The public attributes responsibility to the faculties, and there is often a feeling of great frustration on the part of faculties because of the ridiculous conduct of an amusement enterprise to the damage of the academic enterprise, often without real opportunity for faculty influence to be felt. Similar situations seem now to arise in the South from time to time in relation to desegregation. So, along with my suggestion that we need clear and explicit delegation to put the faculty in certain respects really in a position of authority, there should be adherence to the scheme of delegation even when very critical situations in public relations arise. Institutions should not be committed in large matters of policy without faculty participation.

Comments

2. ALAN K. CAMPBELL
ASSOCIATE PROFESSOR OF POLITICAL SCIENCE,
HOFSTRA COLLEGE

I WOULD BEGIN BY SAYING THAT WHAT WE ARE CONCERNED ABOUT IS not the normal kinds of friction which are created by large-scale organizational structures. Any such organization has frictions. I think if this conference is to serve any function, it is to discover whether or not the tensions that exist in our universities between faculty and administration are something over and above what you would ordinarily expect to find in any large organization. I think the tensions are greater in the colleges, and I believe the reason they are is that the administrators—and as a faculty member I intend to put most of the blame on the administrators—are forced to play many roles.

Whenever I have talked to administrators about this, they always refer to the fact that the faculty is concerned with only one problem, or at most two problems or goals, teaching and research, while the administrator is in the position of having also to face the outside and deal with external problems.

This reminds me of a story which is told of a college president. He was attempting to outline to a convocation the functions of a college president and he pointed out that the president has many problems. He has to present the college to the public. He has to present the college in a favorable light to other presidents. He has to try to inspire the students and, above all, he has to be able to fire faculty members with enthusiasm.

As long as the administrator feels there is a conflict between satisfying the public and satisfying the faculty, there is going to continue to be serious tension. And I would say that what is needed here is for the administrator to look inward again at his university and define rather concretely the goals of his educational institution. I think if he does that, he will come to see—at least I hope he will—that the goals of the college are the goals of the faculty; that is, the discovering and teaching of knowledge. Assuming the administrator accepts these ends as valid, it will be necessary for him to convince the faculty that he sympathizes with these purposes. Furthermore, it is the administrator who must convince the public of the worthiness of these functions. The faculty cannot do it; they do not have the necessary contact with the public.

On many campuses today the faculty feels that the president is not performing this role well. Instead, he often apologizes for his faculty. An individual faculty member gets into trouble because he, as a result of his research and study, comes up with an idea which is not popular with the general public or some special segment of it. There may be pressure brought. I am sympathetic to the administrator who has to face this pressure, but it should be faced with courage, not apologies. I know of an actual instance where the president's reaction in such a situation was to point out to the pressure group that his hands were tied because of tenure regulations and therefore there was nothing he could do. I would argue that the president's function in this situation is to defend the faculty member in terms of the functions of the university. As the leader of that university, he must work for the kind of public understanding which will aid rather than hinder the scholar. Unless he does this, he will not have the respect of his faculty.

Once respect is lost, the faculty is likely to feel the need to protect itself, and it will set up committees which get involved in administration. And the administration is willing to have this happen because it thinks that perhaps, through the committees, it will be able to indicate to the faculty what the administrative problems are and thus get better understanding for them. Some committees may be worthwhile, but they can be and usually are overdone. If the faculty were convinced that the decisions which the administrators are making were decisions in accord with the functions of the university as the faculty sees them, there would be no need for so much faculty participation through committees in administration. Faculty members are not generally much good at administration, anyway, and it takes them away from what they should be doing.

If, as President Wilson said, when a professor becomes a college president he changes his profession, I see very little hope for any lessening of tensions. Particularly if he means that the president ceases to see the educational function in the same way that he saw it as a professor, then I think that there will not be the kind of of accord, rapport, between the faculty and administration which is essential to good education.

I have stated this as bluntly as I can. I realize there is much to be said in opposition to what I have said, but I do believe that what I have said reflects the view of many faculty people and not only the screwballs to whom President Wilson referred.

Comments

3. W. MAX WISE
PROFESSOR OF EDUCATION, TEACHERS COLLEGE,
COLUMBIA UNIVERSITY

IT SEEMS TO ME THE PRESENCE OF STUDENTS INTRODUCES COMPLICA-
tions in the relationships between faculty and administration. As
a member of a faculty, and once an administrator—a dean, it strikes
me that it would be profitable occasionally, when thinking of the
problems of relationships between the faculty and the administration, to take into account that they are both also related in various
ways to members of the student body.

It seems to me that the student bodies on most campuses today
represent a relatively new species. Because students are different
and because they are differently related to faculty and administration than they have been in the past—and differently related to the
public—they complicate the problems we are considering.

There is increased diversity and increased sophistication in college student bodies which add to the burden of forming adequate
relationships on the campus. Relatively few colleges and few college presidents these days make the approach to developing loyalty
in students which was so common thirty years ago, simply because
student bodies have rejected these more obvious approaches. Many
administrators are at a loss to see how they are going to substitute
other devices and other techniques to develop these loyalties. The
attempt may be a hopeless one simply because student bodies are
more splintered in their loyalties than they were in the past. They
have retained much more directly their ties with their local communities and with groups outside the college.

We are apparently in the midst of a period in which we are
redefining the relationship of the college and its students. A study
just after World War II brought out some interesting ideas about
the changing relationship between the professor and the student.
Some of this change in relationship surely was accelerated by the
presence· on most campuses of the World War II veteran, but this
changing relation is, I suspect, a long-term trend. And it puts pres-

sures on both the faculty and the administration which are of a new order.

In relation to this point, some recent studies have been quite interesting in revealing a rather intense sense of urgency in the student body to get to know faculty members better, and a somewhat lower urgency to get to know the administration, particularly the president. If these findings are accurate, they represent some new dimensions in the situation. They may in part reflect student recognition of the rise of the managerial class in the university—I am not making a distinction here between the academic or non-academic, for it isn't only the president who "changes his occupation." Often the dean of the liberal arts college changes his occupation, too, at least in the eyes of the faculty and students, when he ceases to be a professor of history and becomes the dean. He becomes a member of a new class, whether he wishes it or not, which has many of the characteristics of the managerial class in business and industry. The student recognizes this class, and he has certain attitudes toward it which he does not have toward members of the teaching faculty. The fact that the student makes this distinction and treats the two groups differently has a great deal to do with the relationship between the two groups.

Two suggestions for exploring relationships of faculty and administration occur to me.

First, if we are talking about relationships between faculty and administration and if we take into account the student, one useful line of approach would be to discuss what we loosely call the community. A most fruitful approach is to develop communities of administrators, faculty, and students in which there probably wouldn't be more than five or six hundred students, fifty or sixty faculty members, and a very small group of administrators. It is in small groups of this kind, where firsthand contact and acquaintance can be developed, where we can resolve many of the problems we are talking about here today. In a few unique situations the number of students in these communities might rise to a thousand, but these would be most unusual. The idea that faculty and administration and students could be welded into some kind of meaningful relationship with each other in groups of five to ten thousand seems absolutely absurd. The experiments of some universities in radically decentralizing work on their campuses and in developing cohesive administrative-student-faculty communities are, I think, very promising.

Such decentralization may be provided in terms of academic units. It is sometimes done through living units. It could probably be done in other ways. In this connection, I think we have something to learn from the business world. Large business organizations have sometimes been decentralized in such a fashion that something akin to community may be developed.

In many large colleges and universities where there has been decentralization of administration through departments or divisions or schools or other units, there has been no attempt to build a community of faculty, administration, and students. Even within single disciplines we have very frequently organized in ways which make for little sense of community. The department of chemistry in a large university, for example, may include curricular offerings from those of general education for all freshmen through those of the specialized Ph.D. program—a collection of courses in which the freshman may find nothing of meaning to him beyond his present course and one or two professional societies in chemistry whose meetings he may attend.

Some schools provide a different plan, under which faculty members and administrators get together with students in formal and informal ways in developing a community of purpose and interest. Efforts to develop communities in college have a long history in Southern Europe and in Britain. I would not suggest a return to the British residential system, although there is experience with this sort of thing in this country which might be profitable to look at.

A second suggestion, relating to a point made before, is that it would be useful to study the relationships between the faculty and administration as both groups try to relate themselves to the students. I have a feeling, based on observation rather than systematic research, that faculty and administrative groups have sometimes competed for the attention and loyalty of the students. In such competitive situations we find many of our problems. Certainly it is true that many of us who have gone into administration from teaching have bemoaned the fact that "we do not know students" any more, and wish we could get effectively into touch with them.

On the other hand, the efforts of certain members of the administrative staff to establish contacts with the students, often without regard to the relationship of the student to the professor, is a common phenomenon on most campuses.

Comments

4. RICHARD H. SULLIVAN
PRESIDENT, REED COLLEGE

I TAKE IT THERE ARE PERHAPS TWO OR THREE REASONS FOR MY BEING invited to this meeting. First, three years ago I had an opportunity to visit some twenty institutions to study the variety of patterns of relationships and problems that we are here to discuss. Second, I was forewarned that I was to be cast in the role of one who had recently "changed his occupation" by moving into the position of college president. Third, perhaps an element in the invitation was that the institution to which I went seems to demonstrate a difference between the high academic achievement of the place and its lack of administrative orderliness, calm, and continuity.

As I understand it, the interest of the Commission on Instruction and Evaluation in this topic lies not only in the problems of relationship as such but in what influence upon instruction might derive from administrative and faculty relationships. Can we so organize things that everyone is working more efficiently, without the interference of needless frustrations?

I think Reed College is an unusually interesting example. Certainly the administrative discontinuity at Reed has been severe; yet, whatever Reed has accomplished academically has been accomplished under those conditions. I think it is possible to overemphasize the importance of tensions and difficulties that sometimes arise in the relationships of faculty and administration. It may even be that some academic accomplishment of a faculty occurs *because of* tensions that exist. Perhaps a faculty will demonstrate its competence for the purpose of showing a board or an administration that it can do a fine job without having support, direction, and leadership from the board and the president.

It seems to me that one factor that has an important bearing on this problem and that hasn't been mentioned directly is the size of the institution. When it comes to looking for solutions, President Logan Wilson faces a very different kind of situation in attempting to relate himself to a faculty of eight or nine hundred full-time teachers than do those of us in the small colleges in which the president may get to know each faculty member personally—actually may interview every one of them during the course of the year on any variety of topics.

Another factor that I suspect has much importance is very puzzling to me. I think a great deal of what is labeled as tension between the administration and the faculty stems from frictions *within* the faculty. Disagreements between majority and minority groups in a faculty seem to turn themselves into conflicts between faculty and administration, perhaps primarily because the administration seems to have the best chance to do something about these frictions within the faculty. I believe this problem merits consideration in its own right.

The relevance of the economics problem has been mentioned. There never are enough financial resources. Whatever arrangements are made for cooperation between the administration and some representative group from the faculty in making decisions on how to slice limited resources, any such group can be representative only to a degree. Even in a small college it is very difficult to get really effective communication between the entire faculty and the administration in arriving at priorities and budgetary decisions. I think this is a continuing source of tension.

In many institutions personnel policies are obscure. It is very difficult even to find out how personnel decisions are actually made. There is an underlying difficulty in how one is to judge teaching competence and effectiveness. One can go at this by any variety of procedures, but it remains a baffling problem to identify which teachers, among a large group of borderline cases, are to be put in one category and which in another. It is possible, I think, to recognize great teaching and to recognize atrocious teaching. But with respect to the large group in the middle, I think we must assume that no *procedural* solutions are going to remove this basic source of tension.

The board of trustees or board of regents may be a factor in the status of faculty-administration relations. Again, while size may make a difference, in the smaller institutions perhaps a mistake has often been made in keeping the board removed from the life of the academic community. It is possible in various ways to make the board something other than a remote, unknown, and often distrusted body. I recognize that there are some individuals who sit as trustees who basically are antithetic to what the college is trying to do. There has been a lack of courage in many instances in facing this problem and trying to get such trustees removed from our boards. Such persons many contribute far more to these tensions and anxieties than an individual in almost any other position can do.

A final comment might be made on the question of faculty committee assignments. In many cases committee work has been viewed as a chore by everybody, including the administration. All too frequently committees are appointed hastily and mainly to involve people who have not been overworked on other committees. Often if the job to be done is thought through by an administration, it can become an opportunity for a constructive—if quiet and modest— contribution to effective academic performance and a reduction of campus tensions.

Experience in Related Fields—
Parallels and Differences

1. Insights from the Behavioral Sciences

RALPH W. TYLER

DIRECTOR, CENTER FOR ADVANCED STUDY
IN THE BEHAVIORAL SCIENCES

MY ASSIGNMENT TO SPEAK OF SOME OF THE INSIGHTS AND RESEARCH in the behavioral sciences which are relevant to these problems has been made much easier by the comments of previous speakers. Logan Wilson, the sociologist, is a behavioral scientist who used methods of analysis this morning which illustrated the kinds of insights arising from the work of behavioral scientists. T. R. Mc-Connell, psychologist, and Alan Campbell, political scientist, could show us how these problems can be examined by methods of analysis developed by some of the behavioral scientists.

Although the term "behavioral sciences" is increasingly in use today, its meaning is rarely precisely defined. Commonly, it is used as a single term to include all those fields and parts of fields that seek to obtain scientific knowledge of human behavior. Although this is the central concern of such social sciences as psychology, sociology, and anthropology, it also includes parts of every other social science and segments of the biological sciences, such as neurology, ecology, genetics, and physiology. The use of the plural —behavioral sciences—implies what is, in fact, the case, that there is not at present a single science which explains man's behavior as an individual and in all his relations to other men. Although currently efforts are being made to relate the concepts and methods from these various disciplines, no single view has yet emerged adequate for the total range of phenomena considered. An attempt to make a systematic review of developments in all these fields would be superficial both because of time limitations and because of the limitations of my own competence. What I shall do is to pick out a few developments with which I am familiar to illustrate the relevance of the behavioral sciences to an understanding of the problems of relations between faculty and administration.

There are as yet very few scientific studies which have focused upon college and university problems. The publication in 1942 of the volume by Logan Wilson, *The Academic Man*,[1] was an important opening wedge, but this was not followed up systematically until 1956, when the Social Science Research Council sponsored several memoranda outlining possible research programs for the study of higher education as a social institution. These proposed investigations are still only in the discussion stage. Hence, what the behavioral sciences can offer at present are methods and concepts useful in analyzing the situation in colleges and universities and generalizations drawn from other contexts. However, in any particular practical situation, a method for its study will be more productive than any tested conclusions about faculty-administration relations in general. Where improvement is sought, concepts and methods for diagnosing the particular situation provide intelligent and informed bases for action.

To illustrate the possible usefulness of such concepts and methods of analysis, I shall take a few examples of ways in which some of these disciplines look at a particular set of phenomena to suggest how one might examine college and university administrative relations in these terms. Since I can comment on only a few of a larger number of possible models of analysis, these will be only suggestive of a wider range of concepts and methods which could be used.

One of the models used by individual psychologists is helpful in throwing light on the behavior of individual faculty members and individual administrators. In psychological terms an adult individual human being is viewed as an active mechanism whose actions largely follow habit patterns except as these are in conflict with basic needs (drives) or with his values. When such conflicts arise, anxieties develop which are relieved by the acquisition of new behavior patterns by the process of learning. This is a very simple formulation involving only five crucial concepts—habit patterns, basic needs, values, anxieties, learning. Yet it gives one a useful basis for analyzing the situation in seeking to understand the

[1] New York: Oxford University Press.

"inappropriate behavior" of particular individuals. Is the inappropriate behavior due to habit patterns which are inappropriate? Is he satisfying some unmet basic needs? Basic human needs include biological ones, like food, exercise, rest; social ones, like belonging, affection, recognition; and integrative ones, like understanding and control over immediate environment. Is he achieving his values? Does he have unrelieved anxieties? Is he acquiring new behavior patterns by a learning process? If so, are the new patterns, more or less, appropriate ones?

Such a simple, straightforward scheme of analysis does not differ greatly from many common-sense practices used in explaining an individual's behavior. I mention this model here primarily because it serves to link the individual's behavior as an individual to his behavior in the milieu of the college or university. The faculty-administration tensions which are most difficult for most of us to understand are those which are strongly influenced by factors in the college or university situation. Hence, the balance of my comments will be focused on the models for analyzing the college or university as a social institution.

As we move from considering individual behavior in individual terms to individual behavior as influenced by the social context, we are seeking answers to such questions as: What factors in the college or university situation require of the faculty member or the administrator behavior different from established habit patterns? What organizational structures or institutional practices interfere with the faculty member or administrator in his effort to satisfy basic needs or to achieve his major values? What institutional policies and practices stimulate the learning of inappropriate rather than appropriate behavior? To seek the answers to questions like these requires concepts and methods of analysis that can be applied to the college or university as a social institution. Several analytical models have been developed by behavioral scientists which can serve this purpose.

One of these is a model in terms of social structures and their functioning. A college or university may be viewed as a complex social structure which involves not only individual statuses and roles within the institution, but also relationships without. The basic parts of this structure typically include the governing board;

the central administration; administration of college, school, or division; the departments; the student bodies; the alumni; and the professional or academic organizations with which staff members are affiliated.

It is this complex structure, involving ambiguous responsibilities and conflicting expectations, that breeds misunderstanding and dissension. Studies of effective social institutions indicate certain essential characteristics. Each of the members has a clear perception of his role and of his status in the organization. The perceptions of their several roles by the various members of the organization are reasonably congruent.

When the institution is composed of individuals with different abilities and functions and when their effectiveness depends largely on their own exercise of initiative, originality, and judgment, the leadership of the institution depends less on rules and directives for achieving some unity and much more on the development among the members of shared values and purposes.

Furthermore, an effective institution provides rewards for competent performance of roles, and it provides a system of learning which reinforces the acquisition of more effective behavior patterns by the members. It has a two-way communication system which provides both for the development and formulation of policy and directives and also for the feedback which helps the individual to judge the effects of his efforts and to be guided thereby.

The examination of a typical American university will quickly reveal several important respects in which these characteristics for effective institutional functioning are absent or are maintained with difficulty. A faculty member's role as perceived by students is that of teaching; as perceived by the administration it may be that of teaching, of rendering community service, or of research, or some combination of two or all of these; and as perceived by the scientific or scholarly society with which he identifies, it is research. If the faculty member is in a professional field like law or engineering, he encounters further complication of the view of his role as promoting the profession.

It is difficult to develop a sense of common community in a university when some faculty members think of themselves primarily as teachers, some as scholars and scientists, some as lawyers, engineers, business administrators, or physicians, and some as community servants. It is no wonder that confusion and conflict develop over role expectations.

The administrator's role is also an ambiguous one; usually drawn from the academic ranks, he still identifies to some extent with the scientific or scholarly group of which he has long been a member. Working with the governing board and other administrators, his concept of his role is modified to include that of manager, while his contacts with the legislature or private donors and with alumni demand the role of public interpreter of the university. Few administrators formulate for their own guidance a clear outline of the role which they seek to follow which resolves some of these conflicting demands. At the same time, the faculty members have varying views of the administrator's role. Some may think of him as one to provide the financial resources for their work, or to justify the university in the public mind, or to approve their plans for expansion or improvement. Some may view him as the inevitable stern father who denies their every request and frustrates their desires for advancement. Some may carry over the image of him as a faculty colleague, easily sharing their social life and professional concerns. A few will conceive of his role as one of educational leadership, formulating goals and policies and, through exposition and persuasion, gaining wide faculty support of them. In many cases, the same faculty member has conflicting expectations regarding the administrator's role.

There is similar confusion and conflict over the dominant values and purposes of the university. Throughout their graduate training most faculty members were strongly indoctrinated with the values of scholarship, the importance of research, the ultimate significance of new knowledge. Most of them were also impressed with the importance of their own particular field of study and of the relatively minor values of most other fields.

As men and women living in contemporary America, most of them accept some of the current values popular in American life, such as wide public recognition and a comfortable income. From this background many faculty members have not developed great respect for a well-rounded liberal education. They do not idealize the great teacher and want to emulate him. They do not cherish intellectual and aesthetic values. Their goal for the university is more likely to be a great expansion of their own department rather than to be a community of scholars. They are likely to judge excellence in terms of size of faculty, number of students, and level of salaries. They tend to seek promotion and salary increases rather than to focus primarily on becoming more effective as teachers and scholars.

Although this does not complete or exhaust the analysis of the college or university as a complex social structure with its corresponding conflicting effects upon the behavior of faculty members and administrators, it does illustrate the kinds of insights that can be gained by examining a particular college or university situation in these terms.

Two other models of analysis may serve to suggest the variety of concepts and methods which can be used. One of these is commonly called the "social mobility model." This involves the examination of a social institution in terms of the ways in which individuals in it achieve progressively higher levels of respect, recognition, and social status.

In most universities there are several kinds of social mobility. There is the mobility in the system of academic ranks by which an individual faculty member may move from instructor to assistant professor to associate professor to full professor, and perhaps to department chairman, dean, and president. Another kind of social mobility is that obtained through the process of subdividing departments or fields of scholarship, so that the individual in his own special field is supreme. In this way the faculty member becomes a "big shot" by having his own little kingdom of genetics, or astrophysics, or modern English history. A third kind of social mobility is obtained through faculty politics. By getting elected to this committee and that committee, and finally to the university council, a faculty member may achieve wide recognition and status. A fourth kind of social mobility in many colleges and universities is obtained by parties, entertaining, attractive houses, and development of similar extramural skills and resources. A fifth kind of social mobility is obtained through student channels. Some faculty members get increasing recognition through popularity with students. In most colleges and universities, there are fairly well-defined channels for gaining high status with student groups. Other kinds of mobility include opportunities for upward movement through recognition from national, regional, or state professional organizations and opportunities through community services of various sorts.

The significance of analyzing a particular college or university in terms of social mobility lies in the fact that the values of social mobility deeply pervade American society. Most faculty members and administrators are influenced to some extent by desires to increase the amount of respect and recognition they receive. The fact that there are several social mobility ladders available in most institutions is both a source of problems and a means of solution. It may cause faculty-administration conflicts because the administrator may be conscious of only certain of these ladders as being proper directions for faculty members to aspire to, and he may fail to understand the behavior of those faculty members who are devoting time and effort to climbing other ladders. The variety of ladders is also a help in solving problems of tension over social status since a college or university usually has a variety of types of faculty members; the variety of opportunities for upward mobility gives additional avenues for maintaining constructive energy and optimism, whereas, if there were only one status system, that of academic rank, there would be a greater letdown in energy after the full professorship is attained.

Another potentially useful analytical model in examining faculty-administration relationships is the one developed by social psychologists for studying human behavior in small groups. The relative closeness of the relationships in small working groups may partially account for the power of small groups in affecting human behavior. Small groups of this sort often influence individual behavior profoundly as the individual at the same time is influencing the group.

Small working groups are likely to have two foci of attention. One of these is the task it has set for itself, that is, the recognized purpose for which the group exists. The other focus is on the emotionalized social relations within the group. Where the group social relations are under tension, where the individuals are uncertain or unhappy about their status in the group, there is little progress by the group in attaining its recognized purpose, that is, in performing the task it has set. Where group relations are stable and the individuals are clear about their status and find it acceptable, the group morale is high and it is in fine condition for pursuing its basic purposes. Studies of small groups indicate that time is required in the initial stages of a group's activity to establish this stable and effective set of social relations. Some fencing, some preliminary explorations for each member to identify his status and role seem necessary before the group becomes an effective task force. In most colleges and universities, it is likely that a series of analyses of committees and other small task forces would reveal significant differences in social relations between the successful and unsuccessful committees. Such analyses might help lay bare the sources of tensions in those groups which are unproductive. They would suggest some helpful explanations for the sense of futility that often develops with committee work. On the positive side, committees can become an opportunity for productive activity. They can develop a sense of mission and of self-confidence and thus gain greater effectiveness.

These four analytical models for examining faculty-administration relations in a particular college or university are only a few of the fifteen to twenty that are commonly used in the several behavioral sciences. If time permitted we might, for example, consider models related to the decision-making process, reference groups, perception, communication, culture and acculturation, and real and formal power. But I think the four are illustrative of the insights that may be obtained by using concepts and methods of this sort. Some of the implications which arise when using these models to examine a particular college or university situation are immediately evident.

One obvious implication which commonly arises from such analyses is the possibility of reducing tension by capitalizing on the variety of individual talents to be found in all college and university staffs. Unless conscious efforts are made to counteract the effect of departmental government and faculty control over recommendations for appointment and promotion, the pattern will be to select and reward a single type of faculty person and to force out the mavericks who do not conform to the type expectation. Yet, as several of the speakers this morning mentioned, the varied abilities required for effective teaching, research, and community service are not so highly correlated that the person who is easy to get along with is necessarily the greatest scholar or the best teacher or most effective in his public service.

A group enterprise, such as an institution of higher education, requires a range of talents and abilities. The administration is concerned with capitalizing on this range and utilizing the range effectively. This takes ingenuity and continuing effort to identify and reward useful abilities, even when the individual is viewed by his peers as a maverick to be excluded from the faculty community. Often this requires modifications in the academic structure. Too tight a structure means that faculty members who are different can find no place. In such cases, an open structure needs to be developed that provides alternatives to departmental acceptance or membership. When departments get tighter and tighter in a single-track system of status and rewards, it becomes imperative to provide alternative means for distributing rewards and satisfactions to those with useful abilities and alternative structures in which they can work effectively.

A second obvious implication of a social analysis of a typical American university is the need for much greater effort to develop shared values and purposes on the part of the total university. Visits to a dozen major universities and conversations with faculty and administration will clearly indicate sharp differences in the seriousness with which different administrators, even in the same institution, take their responsibility for this important function. It requires continual statement and restatement in many forms and with many concrete illustrations to aid the faculty to formulate and to reinforce its conception of what are the major values of the institution, its significance in society, and the importance of its dedication. This is not something that is done once and for all, because we are all continually receiving conflicting statements of the basic values of the university from newspapers, from alumni, and from other groups. Hence, the pragmatic need for continuing reformulations and reiteration of these important values, not only in general terms, but in terms of particular cases. For example, as each individual case comes up, it is discussed by the administration in terms which bring out the basic purposes and values of the university. In each case the question is raised: How does this relate to our basic values? It is only through continuing efforts to apply them that they become directive·influences for both faculty and administration rather than shibboleths that are repeated periodically for some symbolic occasion.

A third obvious implication arises from an analysis of the behavior of small working groups in a college or university. In many cases the conditions essential for effective work are lacking. There is needed a permissive and relaxed atmosphere, consciousness of and attention to the individual needs of the group, a pace of work which moves as rapidly but no more so than the group is prepared to go, the setting of group goals that can be attained within a reasonable time, and periodic approval for work well done so that the group derives a sense of satisfaction for its efforts. These are conditions the administration can help to provide.

A fourth obvious implication from an analysis of a college or university in terms of a model used by behavioral scientists is the importance of developing both a formal and informal system of two-way communication. Communication serves both an intellectual role and an emotional one. It serves to formulate and guide policies and practices and to stimulate or to relieve tensions. Yet all communication is distorted. Taking the sender's intent as an indication of what should have been communicated and comparing this with the receiver's notion of what was communicated, the distortion is never less than 50 percent, and usually somewhat more. Furthermore, this distortion is selective distortion. The receiver is more likely to get items which help to enhance his ego, or to meet personal needs which are unmet, than he is to get items that have no such personal connection. He is more likely to get items which fit in with his previous notions than items that modify his stereotypes. Studies suggest that the accuracy of communication can be improved by making it a two-way process, in which each person elaborates on what he thinks has been said until there is an agreement on the messages.

Communication among the staff of a college or university serves to stimulate or to relieve tension in several ways. One of these is to provide time for adapting to new situations or new expectations. Recent research indicates that most middle-class people are "living in the future," that is, that their focus of attention is on the periods ahead and with the plans that must be made for them rather than on the present moment. A sudden demand for immediate action which has not been mentally anticipated often proves to be a serious emotional shock. Tensions are reduced by anticipatory communication. This ties in, too, with findings from studies of anxiety in human beings. Fear of the unknown is a frequent source of anxiety. Communication which helps to outline the future so that it is no longer completely unknown serves to relieve tensions. Few administrators have worked out a system of institutional communication with these ideas in mind.

These four implications like the four examples of analytical models for analyzing a particular college or university situation are examples only of the kinds of ideas and suggestions which are likely to arise from applying concepts and methods of the behavioral sciences to the study of faculty-administration relationships. They do not provide a panacea for eliminating problems in this area, but they do provide some of the intellectual equipment which can be used to advantage in seeking to understand and to solve these problems.

2. Insights from Industrial Organization and Relations

H. J. HENEMAN
CRESAP, MC CORMICK AND PAGET

I APPROACH THE SUBJECT WE ARE DISCUSSING HERE WITH RATHER mixed feelings. For about ten years I was a member of a faculty at a large state university. Also in that same university I had some administrative responsibility at the presidential level for a time.

The last ten years I have spent in business. This has meant continued contact with higher education, however, for in recent years one division of our firm has made studies of approximately 140 nonprofit organizations, most of which have been educational institutions or institutions closely related to education, such as libraries and hospitals.

I remember quite clearly the sins of omission and commission of the administration which irritated me when I was a faculty member. I also remember very well how my point of view changed when I got on the other side of the fence and had to assume some administrative responsibility in that university. Experience in business affairs has given me still another perspective regarding the subject we are discussing.

I would like to make several preliminary observations before getting on to more specific points. First, it has been interesting to follow the remarks here today and to see how a subject, which, when narrowly defined, might be regarded as a problem in human relations or administration-faculty relations, has been discussed in broader terms and within the context of very basic problems in management. This is natural and understandable because when we deal with human resources we are dealing with one of the principal elements which concerns top management.

Second, the essentials of top management are much the same in a good many fields. Fundamentally, we are dealing with the organization and utilization of human, physical, and financial resources to achieve certain predetermined objectives.

Third, the management of a university is a more complex job than the management of a business of comparable size. This is a point of view which many trustees often ignore, especially those trustees who are "experts." They are people who need considerable education if they are to perform their role as board members intelligently and constructively.

Fourth, there is often the temptation to believe that solutions to complex or vexing problems in one field can be found by turning to the experience of another field. Some may think that the problem of administration-faculty relations can be cured by some magic formula followed in industry. As attractive as this thought may be, I think it is dangerous to assume that we can find answers to all of our problems in human relationships in the academic world by turning to practices in the business world. I do not believe that practices in private business can be transferred, without change, and applied in our colleges and universities to administration-faculty relations. The business world, too, is searching for answers to problems involving personnel.

For example, take the problem of executive leadership. Someone has referred to the difficulty of finding an adequate number of well-qualified college presidents. The problem of finding good executives is a very real one in the business world. There are not enough outstanding persons to handle the tremendous managerial problems which exist. During World War II and thereafter, these problems grew very much faster than the output of executive talent to deal with them. To be sure, the business world has recognized the need for executive development programs more than has higher education, but both education and industry have the same problem of finding executive talent.

Effective management in higher education is highly desirable, but such management should be responsive and sensitive to the requirements of the educational and research programs which are the chief reasons for a university to exist. Practices from business which can be applied to faculty-administration relationships are few. Business principles which can be applied to the noninstructional areas of university administration are many.

There is no typical organization or typical practice in the business world which can provide definitive solutions to the kinds of problems which prompted this conference. There are well-managed business firms and poorly managed firms, just as there is weak management and effective management among our universities. Some businesses have well-developed programs to eliminate friction in personnel relations at various levels, and some are without such programs.

Because there are some sound business principles which can be applied in certain areas of college and university management, that does not mean that business practices can be transferred to the educational field indiscriminately. There are basic differences which govern those things which are transferrable and distinguish them from those which are not. These include such factors as objectives and organization.

With regard to objectives, those served by an industrial firm usually are more easily identified than goals in the field of higher education. The end product in industry is something which usually can be precisely defined, which is tangible, which is more easily understood by laymen; and it is easier to determine what influences the nature, the use, and the value of this end product. Parenthetically, it might be pointed out that in our studies of college and university management, we have found that many of the problems frequently encountered owe their existence to unclear thinking concerning academic objectives. Many educational organization, budgetary, and personnel problems could be solved if there were a better definition of objectives.

With respect to organization, many business firms have highly integrated and tightly knit organizations. There is something of a command nature in the relationship of a higher level of management to a lower level. In a university, a tightly knit organization, if present at all, is limited to the nonacademic area. In a college or university, there may be actual advantages to loose organization on the academic side for the purpose of encouraging and stimulating freedom of thought and investigation. Scholars should not be curbed by regimentation or strict administrative controls.

In business, the importance of good management is accepted. The role which the president, the vice-presidents, and other officers can play is recognized as being an essential part of the accomplishment of the end objective. There is not always this wide acceptance of top officers in our colleges and universities. Some university presidents are challenged or "second-guessed" constantly by their faculties. Sometimes this is because the contribution which effective administration can make is not clearly understood. In some cases, the top administrative officers themselves are to blame for such a situation because they have been unable to demonstrate that the faculties should be the principal beneficiaries of effective administration.

Colleges may limp along for years with weak or ineffective leadership. A business usually reacts quite rapidly to poor management. Rising costs, lower productivity, shrinking markets, and reduced per-share earnings are among the factors which focus attention on the quality of business management.

In business, greater attention has been directed to the use of certain tools or techniques which can strengthen administration. For example, budgeting is not regarded as something which occurs once each year but is recognized as having a year-round value. The budget is used for planning and programming, for the identification of long-term and short-range objectives, and for controls over operations. Colleges and universities could borrow from business here to great advantage.

In personnel administration, a well-managed business very likely will have a highly developed program to eliminate or to reduce the problems which gave rise to the conference here today. The importance of problems in human relations and of employer-employee relationships are given organizational recognition. There may be a top-level officer who devotes all of his time to personnel administration. There very likely will be programs of executive and professional development. Efforts will be made to identify persons of needed aptitudes, skills, and talents and to develop them through a succession of assignments, opportunities, and training to prepare them to assume more responsible positions in the future.

Persons who fill positions with administrative responsibility are trained and carefully chosen; their selection is not prompted by the difficulty of determining where else to use them. Here is another area where colleges and universities might borrow certain practices and principles which would be to their advantage.

Insofar as it is possible to do so, job responsibilities are defined. Qualifications for positions are determined and criteria and standards are developed against which performance can be evaluated. Salaries and pay plans are established and criteria for advancement are developed and made known. Business finds that these things improve morale.

Many references were made this morning to problems in communication which contribute to human misunderstandings. The well-managed business enterprise recognizes the importance of good communications between top management and various subordinate levels. These communications may vary greatly in nature and content. Some will be oral, some will be written; some will be formal and others will be informal; some will be in the form of staff meetings for certain persons, and others may be in the form of larger conferences. The purposes of these communications will be to explain policies and objectives, to promote loyalty and a "family" feeling, and to develop constructive attitudes on the part of personnel in terms of trying to get as many persons as possible to adopt an over-all point of view as distinct from an individualistic or departmental point of view. In many colleges and universities, the channel of communications could be greatly improved.

No one should realize more than some of you present at this conference how much attention business devotes to improving these techniques of management. Some of you have on your campuses schools or centers of industrial and labor relations for which industry frequently pays a good share of the cost to promote continuous study, investigation, and research for the purpose of finding solutions to some of the problems which this meeting was called to consider. If industry finds such research into its problems to be worthwhile, might it be that the techniques of management in the field of higher education also could be studied to advantage?

Unfortunately, "administration" has been a bad word in a number of colleges and universities. Others here today already have referred to the problems which arise when a faculty and an administration are pitted against each other. Effective management is needed in our colleges and universities. But management is not an end in itself but should serve the academic and research programs. As I already have said, the principal beneficiaries of effective administration should be the faculties. There are many opportunities to strengthen and make more effective those services which support the academic programs.

Finally, there may be a greater disposition in business and industry to recognize and rely upon long-range planning than there is in higher education. It seems to me that here is an area where colleges and universities might profitably borrow from sound business practices. University administrators might discover that many of the problems which exist in their relationships with faculties would be reduced if the objectives of the university are clearly defined and if sound plans have been developed for the purpose of accomplishing these objectives. The objectives and plans should be made known to the faculties so that they might have a greater knowledge of and sense of participation in the future of the university.

3. *Insights from Labor Relations*

RALPH N. CAMPBELL
PROFESSOR OF INDUSTRIAL AND LABOR RELATIONS,
CORNELL UNIVERSITY

IT IS NOT EASY TO CORRELATE LESSONS WHICH ARE LEARNED IN LABOR-management relations with the problem of faculty-administration relationships. There is no general agreement as to what lessons have been learned in the labor-management field. While there are a great many similarities between the two problems, there are also some fundamental differences.

Similarities between Labor-Management and Faculty-Administration Relations

Some of the common features seem to me to be these:

First, in both industrial and educational organizations people are joined together in a cooperative enterprise in which they have both common and conflicting objectives. Since effective organization is based on specialization of function, these people are forced into roles which tend to accentuate their differences and subordinate and obscure their common interests. The personality of the individual, with his unique interests, attitudes, and points of view, tends to be lost in a sterotype of each role. This tendency toward stereotypes further beclouds our thinking about both problems and individuals. Attitudes and emotions develop, addressed to these stereotypes rather than to the realities of behavior. These attitudes and emotions further heighten the conflict and throw up barricades against the intelligent solution of problems.

Through these stereotypes, attention is distracted from the purposes of the cooperative enterprise and focused on the maintenance of status, on the prerogatives of function or role, on the balance of power.

A second similarity is this: in both labor-management and faculty-administration relationships, the personal interest of the employee, if I dare call a faculty member that, centers around wages, working conditions, job security, and status.

In the absence of collective action the individual fears that his interests will be subjected to the caprice of the administrator. In unity he finds strength. The industrial employee may join a union. The faculty member may join the American Federation of Teachers, the American Association of University Professors, or simply seek collective action through his department, college, or university faculty.

The administrator, on the other hand, who is charged with the responsibility for maintaining a proper balance between the conflicting interests of various groups and individuals within the organization as well as between these personal interests and the economic and other goals of the enterprise, would prefer a free hand in dealing with these problems. The frequent result is a battle for control of decision-making in these areas which affect the personal welfare of the individual.

The third similarity I see is that in any large-scale organization—and this has already been mentioned—the resolution of differences becomes complicated by problems of communication. Part of the problem of communication centers around the attitudes and emotions already mentioned; part, around problems of semantics. But a large part of it stems from the sheer organizational distance between those who make decisions, on the one hand, and those who are affected by the decisions, on the other. In every complex organization, therefore, whether it be an educational institution or a business enterprise, a common problem is the development of machinery for effective communication.

These, then, are some of the basic similarities between labor-management and faculty-administration relationships: (1) the tendency to develop stereotyped thinking about roles and to battle over the prerogatives of role or function rather than to seek intelligent solutions of the basic problems of the organization and the individuals in the organization; (2) the struggle for control of decision-making in the areas of wages, working conditions, job security, and status; and (3) problems of developing attitudes and machinery in support of effective communications.

Differences between Labor-Management and Faculty-Administration Relations

A primary difference between labor-management and faculty-administration relationships lies in the authority and responsibility of the faculty of a college or university for the development of educational policy.

The bylaws of Cornell University, which may or may not be typical in this respect, provide that it shall be the function of the faculty to consider questions of educational policy; to determine entrance requirements; to prescribe and define courses of study; to determine the requirements for degrees; to enact and enforce rules for the guidance and supervision of its students in their academic work; and to recommend to the board the establishment, modification, or discontinuance of degrees and the granting of degrees to candidates who have fulfilled the requirements laid down by the faculty.

Let's compare this with industry. In an industrial organization, this would be tantamount to saying that employees are charged with the functions of considering manufacturing policy; recommending the establishment, modification, or discontinuance of product lines; determining the purchasing policies for raw materials; establishing quality standards; and judging whether or not such standards have been met. I know of no instance where management has granted or where employees have demanded such a role.

Even where contracts give labor some voice in such decisions the primary concern of the union is not with these problems per se, but with the impact of these decisions on wages, status, job security, and conditions of work. A university faculty, however, is vitally concerned with educational policy and programming *as such*

Placing such policy-making functions in the hands of a college or university faculty makes the problem of relationships between faculty and administration much more complex than the defining of labor-management prerogatives. It creates a veritable no man's land of authority and responsibility. As one example, how do you separate the administrative budgeting function and allocation of resources from the faculty responsibility for defining curriculum and courses of study?

A second fundamental difference between labor-management relations and faculty-administration relationships lies in the relative freedom of the individual faculty member. Academic freedom requires that the individual faculty member be sovereign as to what and how he shall teach. In an industrial organization, this is tantamount to saying that the individual employee may determine the nature of the product he will produce and the method by which he will produce it. This freedom complicates faculty-administration relationships and puts the administrator under restraints not found in industry.

The nearest counterpart of faculty-administration relationships in the collective bargaining field lies in the unionization of teachers and scientific and technical personnel in industry. A study of the literature concerning organization of teachers and of other professional people indicates that, like other workers, they are interested in having a voice in matters which affect them and in the defense of their self-interests through collective rather than individual action. Two other factors, however, seem to be motivational in the case of both teachers and professional workers: (1) declining income and consequently some decline in status relative to other groups in our society; and (2) failure to have their professional opinions play an important role in determining the policies and operations of their respective organizations.

The desire for individual recognition and the pride of the professional person in his professional responsibility have, when reasonably satisfied, been deterrents to his joining a labor union. When frustrated, however, these motivational forces have been causes of his joining a union.

A third essential difference between administrative-faculty relationships and labor-management relations seems to me to be the availability in the industrial situation of the strike weapon. The workers of an industrial organization can walk off the job without very great fear of severe damage to public confidence in the product of the organization. I don't think this is possible in the case of people who are engaged in educational activity; and, hence, there is a strong deterrent to faculty members' use of the same techniques and strategy which have been useful in the industrial relations field.

This is important because the strike is one of the most effective weapons for reaching agreement in the labor-management relationship. There is no such prime force in most university faculty-administrative relationships. Therefore, we must depend on the insights and good will of the individuals rather than the economic strike for reaching agreement.

The fundamental differences, then, between faculty-administration and labor-management relationships lie in (1) the policy-making role of faculty members as a group and (2) the academic freedom of the faculty member as an individual. These have no true counterparts in industrial organization. These differences are very important to recognize because they complicate the resolution of specific details of faculty-administration relationships. But they do not prevent our applying to such relationships the basic lessons learned from labor-management relations. A third difference I have mentioned is (3) the reluctance of faculty members to use the strike as a bargaining weapon.

Lessons To Be Drawn from Labor-Management Relations Concepts

Now I should like to discuss lessons from the field of labor-management relations which I think are applicable to faculty-administration relationships.

1. Individuals like to know the rules of the game and to be sure that the rules will be applied consistently and impartially. In labor relations this has meant negotiating a labor contract and establishment of grievance machinery to police the contract.

In the case of faculty members, a counterpart would consist of at least a statement setting forth the criteria and the procedures for determining (a) compensation, (b) promotion, (c) workload, (d) amount and type of participation in outside activities, (e) rights to patents, copyrights, and royalties growing out of creative work of the faculty member, and (f) tenure.

Such a statement should be formulated in faculty-administration discussions and not simply announced unilaterally by administrative officers. The individual who feels that he has a grievance growing out of a violation of policies or procedures set forth in the statement should have recourse to some form of grievance procedure, perhaps a hearing before a faculty personnel committee and the administrative officer concerned.

2. Most effective labor-management relations have developed where the issue of prerogatives has not been permitted to develop and where neither party has adopted a legalistic approach. Studies by the National Planning Association on the *Causes of Industrial*

Peace[1] indicate that a common practice by management, in cases of constructive relationships, is to consult with the union before introducing any significant changes and by this means to avoid a showdown on the question of prerogatives. Where this has happened the union, in turn, has tended to be constructive rather than to insist on its prerogatives. Corollary to this is the finding that in the most positive relationships negotiations tend to be problem-centered; that is, more time is spent on specific problems rather than in defining abstract principles. Intelligent compromise is the order of the day.

To the harried college administrator who is concerned with problems of budgets, with fund raising, and with public, alumni, and governmental relationships, the time and patience required for such consultation may seem unjustified. In the absence of time for adequate consultation, however, it seems to me that the minimum to settle for is the delegation of authority and responsibility to someone other than the president, and to see to it that he has, in fact, the authority and responsibility to make decisions.

Time spent in hammering out basic policies and procedures will probably be more than offset by the elimination of specific problems as well as basic conflicts and frustrations which result from a failure to reach agreement on fundamental policies and procedures.

Faculty members who concern themselves with abstract principle may find the idea of compromise repugnant and perhaps immoral. Intelligent compromise, however, need not mean the surrender of basic objectives by either party. As Mary Parker Follett, so well known for her pioneering ideas in the field of organization and administration, has pointed out, the essence of effective decision-making in any conflict of interest lies in finding new solutions which can satisfy the basic objectives of all concerned.

3. A third lesson we can learn is that in effective relationships, grievances are settled promptly and as close to the point of supervison as possible. There is flexibility and informality within the grievance procedure, and the grievance machinery is used to deter-

---

[1] The lessons cited here and in item 4 have been drawn from Clinton S. Golden and Virginia Parker (ed.), *Causes of Industrial Peace: Under Collective Bargaining,* Case Studies No. 14, National Planning Association (New York: Harper & Bros., 1955). See especially pp. 93-94.

mine trouble areas and then to work toward the prevention of grievances.

This suggests that in large universities personnel problems be settled promptly at the department, or at least at the school or college level. This calls for machinery at such levels to deal with problems as they arise within the framework of the criteria and procedures I have already mentioned. There should be, of course, the right of appeal to university-wide authority.

4. A fourth lesson is that there is in most effective labor-management relations widespread union-management consultation and highly developed information sharing. The union can, of course, provide effective machinery for management communications with the worker only when the labor-management relationship is generally constructive rather than antagonistic. Where the relationship is cooperative and the union assumes responsibility for keeping workers informed, it can provide a very effective channel for communications.

In the university, machinery for communications exists in such agencies as faculty committees, faculty representation on boards of trustees, and in certain administrative offices, such as that of provost, dean of the faculty, and college deans and department heads.

However, with regard to these offices, it seems to me that the selection for ability to carry on communications should be an important part of the selection process. What actually happens, however, where relationships are deteriorating, is a struggle in which the faculty would like to see in these positions individuals who represent the extreme points of view of the faculty, while the administrative officials would like to see those individuals who are most closely aligned with the administrative point of view. I suggest that what is really required are individuals who can bridge the gap, and it is to the advantage of both the administration and the faculty to see that such persons are selected for these positions.

Another lesson in constructive labor-management relations is that there is full acceptance by the management of the collective bargaining process and of unionism as an institution and that the company considers a strong union an asset to management. On the other hand, the union fully accepts private ownership and operation of the industry and recognizes that the welfare of its members depends upon the successful operation of the business. Mutual trust and confidence exist between the parties.

This suggests that for effective faculty-administration relationships there should be a recognition of the importance of the role of each and a respect for that role. Faculty members cannot look on administration as a necessary—and sometimes unnecessary—evil. Nor can administration look on faculty members as prima donnas whose prime tendency is to interfere with the smooth functioning of the administrative process. Unfortunately, where undue emphasis is placed on role, function, and prerogatives, the picture I have just painted of faculty and administration tends to be at least partly true.

Up to this point I have placed little emphasis on systems and techniques largely because I mistrust techniques where the more fundamental qualities of effective relationships are missing. As Alexander Pope has said, "For forms of government let fools contest; whate'er is best administer'd is best."

I do want to depart here from the general tenor of my remarks to discuss one specific aspect of personnel policy. In industry and in the public school system the route to success, higher compensation, and prestige has been via the move from teaching, engineering, or research to administrative positions. Outstanding teachers, engineers, and scientists have become poor administrators because this was the only route to advancement. As long as administrators establish the salary systems they will have a natural tendency to give highest status to administration.

In industry there is a developing tendency to establish a dual route for promotion—for supervisory and administrative personnel, on the one hand, and for engineering and scientific personnel, on the other. One union contract specifies there will be no top salary limitation for personnel engaged in scientific activities.

Universities might pay more attention to this possibility of solving some of the dilemma. Of course, endowed chairs now provide satisfactory compensation for some outstanding faculty members.

I would like to underscore in my comments what has already been said, that in labor-management relations as well as in university administration, conflict is not necessarily bad. When we no longer have differences of opinion, the primary role of an educational institution will be lost. With some conflict inevitable, then, pressures are created for both faculty members and administrators to try to resolve their mutual problems through some of the attitudes and approaches that I have suggested here.

4. *Insights from Public Administration*

YORK WILLBERN

PROFESSOR OF POLITICAL SCIENCE; DIRECTOR, BUREAU OF PUBLIC ADMINISTRATION, UNIVERSITY OF ALABAMA

WE WERE ASKED TO TALK ABOUT INSIGHTS AND RESEARCH IN RELATED fields which may have relevance for the identification, analysis, and solution of basic problems of faculty-administration relations. I was asked to cover the field of public administration. My comments concern a great deal of analysis, more or less acute, by observers of public administration agencies; to say that these are research findings would be stretching the fact.

Colleges and universities in this country have become bureaucracies of considerable size. The faculty of a contemporary college or university is ordinarily much too large to constitute an effective face-to-face group. The operating face-to-face group nowadays is the academic department or, in some cases, the faculty of a small professional school. These units frequently develop a very powerful cohesion and group spirit. They are the "in" group in the institution; other groups, generally speaking, are the "out" groups.

Sometimes these small groupings identify themselves with a larger unit, the college or university; sometimes not. Within such actual work groups there may sometimes be, of course, some dissatisfaction with department chairmen, but this is a personal matter rather than a dichotomy between us and the administration—"us" being the faculty.

To some degree the administrative personnel, particularly since we generally have separate administration buildings for such personnel, constitute themselves a separate definable work group.

It is these actual operating work groups which constitute the effective building blocks of organization and activity. Rarely are the central administrative officials of a university considered to be in the same work group as teaching members of the faculty. Administrative officers are considered to be outsiders by most teachers. When they constitute themselves, through personal and social contacts and relationships and frequent work contacts, a clearly identifiable separate work group, this feeling of separateness is accentuated.

Another feature which increases the "distance" between administrators and faculty is the way in which policy decisions are made. In a large organization decision-making becomes institutionalized and, to persons necessarily excluded from part or all of the process, impersonal and even hidden. The president considers "our" recommendations by conferring with someone else about them, or even referring them to someone else, and the persons primarily affected feel left out. A feeling of belonging exists only if there is a feeling of participation in decision-making, and this is hard to arrange in a larger organization.

Furthermore, a bureaucracy of considerable size has a difficult problem of internal communication, a subject that has received a considerable amount of attention by students of public administration. Formal and informal communication both become very important. There need to be ways of collecting information and of distributing it and of arranging for "feedback," so that there will be some reaction to information communicated in either direction. Faculty meetings, senates, councils, committees, reports, regular bulletins or "house organs," and particularly the college newspaper, become channels for both communication and the social process of decision-making. It might be suggested that there is a very high negative correlation between the degree of internal communication and the amount of friction between faculty and administration.

Before I leave the matter of size, which I think is at the root of part of our problems of faculty-administration relations, I would like to say this. When Mr. Campbell suggested this morning that he thought the frictions between faculty and administration in a mod-

ern college or university were greater than in a similarly large group
of another type, I was a little startled because I was not sure I
agreed. I would have said an academic community tended to be
a generally happier and better related community. Certainly, as
President Wilson said, most faculty members like the environment
and want to stay in it. Mr. Campbell may be right, however. It may
be that the frictions are greater in an academic community than in
a similarly large bureaucracy, whether public or private, of another
kind.

One reason why they may be getting greater is that the higher
educational institutions are in a process of rather rapid institutional
change. In the past they have been and were traditionally communities of scholars in which the scholars felt, as President Wilson
said, substantially equal, and in which the necessity of group activities was minimal, in which each man did his own work, and co-
operated with others only slightly. But in recent years—and presumably even more in the future—our educational institutions are
becoming producers of products which are strongly demanded so-
cially and are in short supply, with an increase in production expected. We are asked to turn out more students and more research
and more services and more adult education and more television
programs, with resources more and more inadequate to meet these
demands for products.

With that kind of pressure, we have had to introduce various
elements of control and direction and management. The scholars
are being manipulated. We have had to do this in order to try to
adapt limited resources to expanding needs. This has produced, I
think, some tensions and some frictions greater than university
communities have had in the past.

It is in a time when an institution is changing from one pattern
to another pattern that the tensions become most pronounced. This
is when the role expectations are under stress, when you don't have
the same job that traditionally you had before or that you thought
you were going to have when you took it.

Management of the faculty community may become even more
necessary in the future, because our resources to meet the demands
put upon us will be increasingly inadequate. Therefore, there will
be pressure to be sure that we are using these resources in the most

efficient possible way; we will be expected to maximize our output with the resources we have.

In a large bureaucracy, there appear ordinarily certain work group "survival techniques" which create strain between top officials in administration and work units. Areas of work are jealously guarded, empires are built, possible surpluses of staff and space are concealed. As a department head I have learned a good many techniques by which you can keep the administration from knowing when you have a little fat in one place or another. For the work group, this is highly desirable, because next year we may need it and if we sacrifice it this year, we are not likely to get it back next year.

Since members of the administration are considered outsiders and incapable of judging accurately the relative merits of insiders, seniority is frequently defended as a basis for advancement. Administrative proposals that promotion and salary increases be based upon merit are considered by many working members of the faculty to be an attempt to exercise arbitrary discrimination.This is particularly true in an academic community with a long tradition of equality among scholars. Administrators feel, of course, that it is a great waste of limited resources to spread them across the board on any such basis as seniority.

Organizational arrangements, which must be formalized at least to some degree in a large bureaucracy, can help or hinder communication and cooperation. Since size is at the root of many of these difficulties in communication and understanding, there is apparently much to be said for decentralization, which has been suggested here by others, for having faculties rather than a faculty, for leaving as much as possible to each division or department, even though this results in diversity rather than uniformity. This is not to say, of course, that decentralization doesn't have its problems. One of my colleagues in public administration, talking about decentralization in government, says that you must always remember that, before you can decentralize, you must be centralized, and educational institutions have not always reached the first step.

One of the oldest areas of technical improvement in the field of public administration has been the development of central staff agencies for accounting, for purchasing, property control, public relations, long-range planning, and so forth; to organize these separately with centralized agencies to handle the functions for the whole community is an arrangement by which economy and efficiency presumably can be promoted.

These central management agencies have all developed in colleges and universities along with special agencies for unique educational functions—student record-keeping, student counseling and guidance, the library, contract research development, and various public-service activities, such as extension, and so forth.

These central agencies are designed to provide service to the operating units, the units which perform the teaching and research which are the major functions of the university. Service and control become mixed, however. When the librarian decides that money can be used for separate titles but not multiple copies of the same title, who is determining the instructional policy of the institution? Friction with the business office is frequent if not continual. Many faculty members feel that the business office, or the records office, has easier access to the president than they have. Physically it is nearly always arranged that way; the business office is in the same building and adjacent to the president, and the comptroller goes into the president's office to see him regularly, and no faculty member sees him at all.

With regard to the policies of these central offices, of course, the size of an institution produces at least a fancied need for uniformity. All secretarial desks must cost the same; travel is not permissible for one if it has been denied for another who is similarly situated. Such matters are not always easy for faculty members to understand.

A faculty member is subject to dual, if not multiple, supervision, with instructions coming from the registrar about some matters, the dean about some matters, the department head about other matters, the library about still other matters. The administration becomes "them," the teachers "us."

This makes the role of middle management, the department heads and the deans, crucial in attempting to straddle the gap. I think particularly the department chairmen have an extremely important place. It is comparable to the role of foreman in industry, although I am sure they would not like that comparison. They must be part one and part the other.

One of the chief areas of study for students of public administration has been the central role of the chief executive, in this case the college or university president or chancellor. He must be the representative of the general interest, attempting to reconcile the differences of specialists, whether they be subject-matter specialists or staff or administrative specialists. The characteristics and qualities of leadership at this level are difficult of definition but of incalculable importance.

In the larger institutions, of course, it has become the presidency rather than the president. The chief executive must be institutionalized. If there are any points about which public administrators agree, one of them is that it is false economy to deny the chief executive of a large institution adequate staff assistance. Of course, the employment of these staff assistants is generally automatic with the growth of the institution. Whether they are vice presidents, provosts, administrative or academic assistants, or whatever the title, they must share in the operation and responsibilities of the central executive office.

They are necessary, yet they increase the problem which has been suggested here before of distance between the man who is actually doing the work of the university and the man on whom the responsibility for the university performance primarily rests.

A group that is highly professionalized appears to be much harder to control from a central position, whether it is in government or elsewhere. In this characteristic, of course, higher education is at the top of the list. Institutions of higher education go nearly as far back in history as the church, and have been from time to time nearly as independent; and the independence of the institutions has its counterpart in the independence of the faculties. An independent professional man is hard to control or administer, yet control and administration become more and more necessary as institutions grow larger, as we are called upon to do more things with bigger institutions and less adequate resources.

Professionalization in higher education has come to mean increasingly the professionalization of specialists, as the disciplines have splintered and multiplied. This is a problem which, in general public administration, has been met in part by a still slight but discernible growth of professionalized generalists. The city manager is a generalist as compared to a fire chief, and he is developing a very respectable profession. In higher education, as has been remarked earlier, there has been little concern for any such professionalization of the university or college administrator.

Students of public administration of the current generation have come to realize fully that public administration is a political process, that it is immersed in politics, and that there is politics from the bottom to the top. Certainly a college campus is no exception to this generalization. There is a constant tug and haul of competing forces, a constant struggle for influence and prestige.

In the political process of administration, many things must be taken into account, many reactions must be anticipated. The administration of an institution of learning has several constituencies—the students, alumni, parents, the legislature if it is a public institution, prospective donors, the general public, as well as the faculty. The administration has the taxing role of trying to respond to each of these constituencies and to represent one to the others. It is an extremely difficult job to be responsible and representative with regard to all.

It may be impossible to turn the same face to all groups. The administration would want the faculty to know, for example, that space was being inadequately utilized, but would have some reluctance in sharing this information with a legislature. The existence of these different constituencies complicates and confuses the problem of communication. What can be told to one group without disturbing another unnecessarily?

One of my colleagues was saying in a faculty group the other day that all that was really needed was for the public to be better informed about what the university was about and what it was doing. There was a lack of communication between the university and the public. Another faculty member, with some but not too much overstatement, replied that this would be the most dangerous thing that could happen: "If the public of this state knew what we are actually doing at this university, they probably wouldn't want it." The administration must interpret to all groups, depending on their background and ideas and goals and interests.

Some faculty groups learn that their political power is greatly increased if they can be identified with clientele groups. The professional schools have a great advantage over the academic faculties in this respect. I might cite law, engineering, and medicine, for example. The faculty will associate itself with the professional group, and then they speak not only with the voice of the faculty but with the voice of the organized profession, and the administration must recognize the pressures from both.

Underlying all these problems is the question of motivation, or the incentives that produce cooperative endeavor. The question of what leads a man to cooperate or not to cooperate in an organization is one that has been central to the study of both business management and public administration. A man who has contributed much to recent thinking in this matter is Chester Barnard, although there were earlier persons whose thinking went in the same channel, and others who have developed and amplified it since.

According to Barnard, authority comes from below, not above. As he says, "Under this definition the decision as to whether an order has authority or not lies with the persons to whom it is addressed, and does not reside in 'persons of authority' or those who issue these orders." To illustrate what he means in striking fashion, he quotes Major General James G. Harbord as to "the inarticulate vote that is instantly taken by masses of men when the order comes to move forward. . . . The Army does not move forward until the motion has 'carried.'"

Most students of the subject now agree that organizational incentives are only partially economic, and that economic motivations have been greatly overrated. This may be particularly true of faculty members, which is not to say, of course, that economic incentives can be completely ignored. Other factors which are frequently not given sufficient weight by administrators in higher education, as well as in other organizations, are opportunities for distinction, prestige, and personal power and influence and desirable physical conditions of work—clean, quiet surroundings, for example, or a private office. How many people of comparable professional standards would have to walk down to the end of the hall to answer a telephone, as many professors have to do? Other incentives are comfort and satisfaction in the social relationships of the organization; familiarity with, and acceptance of, the customs and behavior patterns of the organization; and feeling of participation in large and important events.

A good many studies of public agencies have indicated the overwhelming importance of a sense of significant mission in the securing of internal cooperation and relative effectiveness. Some of the pioneering agencies of the New Deal, most of the emergency and war agencies of the early 1940's, the Tennessee Valley Authority for a twenty-year period, have had tremendously high internal cohesion and morale largely because there was a sense of participation in a great enterprise. Studies which have been made for the Air Force indicate the great increase in cooperativeness which occurs in emergency periods, or even in simulated battle exercises, as compared to routine peacetime training. When the goal is known and accepted, group spirit produces a high degree of willing participation. The difficulty is to create this sense or illusion of high purpose.

Institutions of higher education have some advantage over other large bureaucracies. Professors have had a sense of dignity, prestige, professional worth, and participation in a high calling which has not always been present in other bureaucratic environments. One of my colleagues in public administration has called the administration of higher education a "happy chaos." It may be that, as the pressure of events has required us to cut down somewhat on the chaos, we have tended also to cut down on the happiness.

Selections from the Discussion

Impact of Forces Outside the Institution

PROFESSOR PETRY: I wouldn't expect to prevent tension between faculties and administrations, but I am concerned with what seems to me to be a tendency to make college organization more and more in the image of either a military or a business machine. That is going to destroy education.

PROFESSOR RALPH N. CAMPBELL: We stress too much the difference between an educational institution and a business organization. The very problem that Professor Petry has been pointing out between the academic and nonacademic staff in a university is exactly the fight that has been going on in industry between the line and the technical staff organization. The problem of the specialist in a particular area who does not understand the basic functions of the business is just as acute in many industrial organizations as it is in the academic institution.

CHAIRMAN ELMER ELLIS (President, University of Missouri): I think part of the problem is the growth of our institutions, greater specialization within them, and greater diversification of our functions. These go on all the time. Looking back in the history of our own institution, fifty years ago if a student wanted to change a course, his case came before the full faculty. They voted on a student request to shift from one course to another. You might say that was complete faculty government. Thank heaven we don't bother with that any more.

But where to stop in centralization? Where to stop in bringing in specialized people to handle certain functions that formerly were handled by the faculty or by faculty committees?

PROFESSOR FUCHS: Take the matter of counseling. We have to have specialists in counseling, and we are getting them at a great rate. But a faculty attitude of considerable superciliousness toward the counselor has developed. I believe this problem runs through all our operations.

PRESIDENT O. C. ADERHOLD (University of Georgia): It seems to

66

me that most tensions in our institutions grow out of rules and regulations and laws that are beyond the realm of the institution itself. Regulations on centralized purchasing, for instance, and the machinery that is set up by state governments to deal with it are a constant irritation. Sometimes state laws are the problem. At our institution, for example, for five or six years we went through the drudgery and irritant of working with quarterly budgets. There was nothing at the time that we could do about it. If you add to that the security questionnaires and oaths that are required, regulations of the Federal Government on contract research and grants—if you add all of these together, it's a wonder that we keep either the faculty or the business office happy.

The tendency is to blame all of this on the business office, though there isn't a thing in the world the business office can do except to carry out these regulations and laws. You can try to explain it, but that doesn't keep the average faculty member from criticizing the officers who have the responsibility for carrying out the regulations.

CHAIRMAN ELLIS: I was thinking you might have added to that the questionnaires we send each other.

PRESIDENT ADERHOLD: I have found a way of disposing of that.

PROFESSOR ALAN K. CAMPBELL: I would like to say a word about the young faculty member in this connection. A particular kind of tension in the junior ranks is created by the fact that education has become a national issue and that the teacher in particular is receiving a great amount of publicity, especially on the problem of salary levels.

Higher faculty salaries would be welcomed by all, but I believe this is not the basic problem. I believe it is the setting in which this issue is fought—the spirit of the times—that represents the essential problem.

The young faculty member did his graduate work under a number of professors, for some of whom he developed friendship, fondness, and great respect. He looked upon their role in society as a very important role, so important in fact that he wanted to assume that kind of role himself. Then he became a faculty member. Now he reads about how low his pay is in relation to other professions. And, having developed as a graduate student a somewhat idealized version of the "society of scholars," he finds this version a bit short of reality. There are the same kinds of problems in human relations there that exist in other organizations.

The thing that makes it really tough for him is that he is young enough to get out, and he often has the opportunity to do so. Many of my friends have gotten out. They are making $15,000 to $20,000 a year if they have gone into private business, and between $10,000 and $15,000 if they have gone into government, which is where people in my own field have gone. Many of those who left now wish they had not. But my point is that while they were on campus they found it difficult to apply themselves because they felt the constant pressures of public attention and internal turmoil.

The faculty member has doubts about the public attitude toward his work. Is it really worthwhile? The very fact of low salaries, with all the attendant publicity, is perhaps one of the key pieces of evidence that their function is not respected by the community.

I think the leadership which the administration gives, and particularly the president, is very important at this point. If only some way could be found to reassert the importance of this function. It can't be done by speeches. It has to be done concretely. And it has to be done if we are going to keep our young faculty. One of the reasons for much of the tension is the fact that the young people really see alternatives and they are constantly asking themselves, shall I stay, or shall I get out?

The Relation of "Businesslike Management" to Academic Efficiency

PROVOST WILLIAM C. FELS (Associate Provost, Columbia University): In business and industry there is a noticeable relationship between good management and productivity. Is there any evidence that there is such a relationship in academic institutions?

MR. HENEMAN: I don't know how you can measure productivity from an educational standpoint.

PROVOST FELS: You don't know how to measure it?

MR. HENEMAN: What is an educated man, for example?

PROVOST FELS: You do not, I think, measure productivity always in terms of what an educated man is, although there have been some efforts to do that. But if your argument is that management can somehow contribute to the productivity of the faculty, there ought somewhere to be some evidence that good management *does* contribute to this. I am not sure that there is a relationship. But I think it would be very important to know whether there is any before one embarked on such a businesslike management for a university.

PROFESSOR WILLBERN: It was suggested that certain institutions have had good results with poor management. I don't agree with this. There may not have been good management according to a given definition. But from whatever source it came—maybe from the faculty—the management has been good.

PRESIDENT SULLIVAN: That begs the question somewhat. Our discussion of management has been largely in the context of management by the administration. If you say good management can occur with a terrible administration because the faculty manages it well, that is something else again—though this has happened.

PROVOST FELS: Could we introduce a term, "businesslike management"? Do we find that academic productivity is the result of businesslike management?

MR. HENEMAN: I wouldn't necessarily try to relate those two. You can go at it the other way.

PRESIDENT M. D. WHITAKER (Lehigh University): You can increase faculty salaries by businesslike management of the business end.

PROVOST FELS: Businesslike management of the business end, as has been pointed out here, intrudes on the faculty and can be a source of friction between the administration and faculty.

MR. HENEMAN: It shouldn't be. This depends on what is in your mind when you think of businesslike management, but I don't see why businesslike management should result in friction with the faculty. Problems can grow out of poor management. Businesslike management, properly conceived, is something that should be serving faculty needs.

PROVOST FELS: All right, eliminate the business activities from the businesslike management question. Does businesslike management contribute to the productivity of faculties?

MR. HENEMAN: I don't know whether it does or does not. It can contribute to better faculty morale if you have the organization more clearly defined, have introduced sound planning, have operations running smoothly, and if the supporting services rendered to teaching and research programs are prompt and effective. You can contribute better services, you can contribute higher salaries. Maybe these things do increase productivity, I don't know. But I think it would be a mistake to try to measure productivity of the faculty the way you would measure output of the Chevrolet plant.

PROFESSOR RALPH N. CAMPBELL: I think we are in difficulty as long as we stay at the level of generalities. Let's take a specific example: the relationship of the budgeting process to curriculum development. Here, there is a definite relationship between the problems of business management and the educational program. I think no one would suggest that a president of an institution should continue indefinitely to run a university on a deficit. So you get into the question, then, given the educational mission of the university, what is the best allocation of resources? In my opinion, the most effective manager is the individual who can work with the faculty in determining what the educational mission is and what allocation of resources is best going to contribute to this mission. In doing so, the manager certainly has a role to play in the productivity of the faculty.

Role of the U.S. College President

MISS NANCY DUKE LEWIS (Dean, Pembroke College, Brown University): It is difficult to find a man who can run the physical plant and the budget and mechanics of a university efficiently and who can also tolerate a loose organization among faculty. It is hard for the same kind of mind to accept the two.

PRESIDENT WILSON: I think also you have the problem of the allocation of the president's time. He can readily be misunderstood by the faculty. I am sure a lot of my faculty feel that I don't spend enough time sitting down with them to discuss educational policy and so on. Well, I enjoy doing that very much. That is the old-fashioned conception of what a university president is supposed to do.

But there are other people on our staff who do that—the deans, the vice-presidents, and so on. The problem is that there are certain contacts in which it is either the president or no one. If he doesn't do it, it doesn't get done. And I feel that I can be of more value to our faculty by spending my time on those matters. There are just so many hours in the day, and that is something else they are reluctant to accept, that you cannot keep cutting yourself into smaller and smaller pieces. I believe I serve the university better and the faculty better by concentrating on some of these "outside" functions.

I can think of a university president who is well known for his utterances, his essays, and so on. I don't know whether he was a great university president or not. He was head of his institution a long time. When he left, the endowment was about the same as it was when he went there. Increasing the endowment is an extremely important thing in a private institution. I feel he probably would have served his institution better if he had foregone some of these essays and had spent a lot more time on this other matter. It is true we read his essays with great delight and interest, but they did take much away from his time that could have been spent otherwise.

Again, in the budgetary matter, the faculty can easily misunderstand that. Budgetary controls save money for salaries if they are properly attended to.

PRESIDENT WHITAKER: I couldn't agree more with what has been said. There is a general misconception of the role of a college president. The role that is present in the public mind and in many faculty minds is a role that might have been possible with a student body of three or four hundred, but it is completely impossible now.

Furthermore, you cannot properly delegate authority which has been centered in the president, in the way that has been preached this morning by many of us and, at the same time, have no one standing between the faculty member and the president, which has also been preached.

PROFESSOR T. R. McCONNELL (School of Education, University of California, Berkeley): On this last point, it seems to me that there are various ways to organize an administrative group so that you can hold the distance between the teaching staff and the top administrative staff to the smallest possible "psychological distance." A staff may be organized on a line system almost entirely, with a hierarchy of line administration that gets very long after a while. But I think it is possible to organize an administrative group in other ways that tend to hold this distance down rather than to increase it. This is one thing that might well be studied.

DEAN LEONARD BEACH (Graduate School, Vanderbilt University):

There is one other thing that I have been listening for and haven't heard. I wonder whether we made an initial distinction between the different kinds of top executives. A college president may be a magnificent leader—a courageous, far-sighted, top general—and this same leader may be a poor manager; and sometimes progress is made by this kind of leader. The problem that may result in this situation arises from the "filters," or the intermediate officers, who convey or attempt to convey some of the messages from the leader down into the ranks. I think we would be much less well off than we now are if we had not had some of this kind of educational leadership.

DR. TYLER: You can generalize the problem of the presidency or whatever you call the top administrative officer. The position is really so stupendous that nobody ever fills it completely. If you look at the office historically, there are two kinds of approach. One is to round it out by building an office in which responsibility is shared among a number of persons. The other one is to alternate administrators so that in one period of time an institution is strong in one aspect of administration, then moves to another period when it gains different kinds of strength by having another kind of administrator. But one never has at one time all the qualities one would like to have in the central administration.

PROFESSOR McCONNELL: This is a good hint on which to go. The contribution of a given man might be more in one direction than another, and it would be undesirable to have administrators stay too long.

PROFESSOR RALPH N. CAMPBELL: I would like to come back to the question of leadership. The behavioral scientists have made some progress in the study of leadership, but they have tended to focus on the role of an individual and his own traits. There has been very little in the way of study of the organizational teams which actually manage the institutions—it is never one individual. I think it would be very helpful if we have some studies of what kinds of teams tend to be most successful in the management of institutions and what relationships develop within them which make them most effective.

PRESIDENT WILSON: I think you put your finger on something important. Some of the most publicized university presidents in my book haven't done their institutions too much good, however much fame they built up for themselves personally. There are others who are less well known and who meet the pragmatic test of having accomplished a good deal for their institutions. The secret may be that they were more self-effacing, more of the teamwork type, not concerned to be out on the stage all the time. They built a real team to do what, in a large university, is necessarily a team job.

PROFESSOR RALPH N. CAMPBELL: The problem for the chief involves picking executive people who are different from himself to fill the gaps in his own skills, and getting along with them. I don't think there are many studies of this.

PROFESSOR ALAN K. CAMPBELL: There is one comment I would like to make. I am bothered by what has been said about the leadership role of the college president. I am particularly disturbed by a couple of remarks President Wilson made about the great load upon the college president today. The accuracy of his description I do not question. A senior American historian of national reputation spoke for a great many faculty people the other evening, when he said at a small faculty gathering that in his judgment the biggest difference in the educational world today as compared to twenty-five years ago is today's lack of educational leadership. I think the reason for this is that the college president has been given so many jobs to do that he cannot possibly do them all, and the ones that have fallen by the wayside are those related to academic leadership.

We know that in any large-scale organization there is a tendency to push more and more power and responsibility onto the executive. That certainly has been our experience in the public field. The result in American government is the institutionalization of the presidency which has provided the President with much staff assistance. I hope this will happen in higher education so that the college president will have time occasionally to sit back and think and perhaps even write an essay.

It is, in fact, unfortunate that our college presidents don't write more essays. Certainly I don't want them to stop raising money, either. But the faculty feels this lack of intellectual leadership, and feels it because such leadership cannot come from the faculty. The faculty is made up of specialists. They become leaders in history, in political science, in chemistry, but they do not become leaders in education. They are looking for real academic leadership. If we are going to get it, it will have to come from the president. Of all the functions of the college president this is one that cannot be delegated.

CHAIRMAN ELLIS: There is a definition of the president's job, said to have been offered by a student on our campus—I presume it is told on others, too: "The president's job is to make speeches. The faculty's job is to think. The dean's job is to keep the president from thinking and the faculty from making speeches."

Academic Preparation of College Presidents

PROFESSOR MCCONNELL: I was going to ask [Professor Willbern] whether he believes that the idea that public administrators should be trained in general administration ought to be applied to university and college administrators.

PROFESSOR WILLBERN: I was speculating on that. I don't have a definite opinion on it. It does impress me that our faculty members are educated as historians, biologists, and what not, and there is no good way that they can be educated about general problems of education at higher educational institutions, other than in meetings like this to which most of them never go.

PROFESSOR MCCONNELL: One of my associates points out that in public administration this idea of the generally trained administrator is growing. Some of the professional staffs, for example in departments of public health, have come to the conclusion that their administrative officer should be a general administrator rather than a professionally trained man in medicine or health sciences. If this idea were applied to university administration, it would be, I take it, a very great revolution.

PROFESSOR WILLBERN: This is not going to happen, at least at any specific point in time. I would not propose that but something short of that, in which there is some attempt to involve faculty members in the problems of general administration. Presumably out of this some "specialists in general administration" could be produced. I don't see any likelihood of departments of higher education in a few of our top institutions training the presidents of institutions around the country.

PROFESSOR MCCONNELL: I may say that I have a deep suspicion of the idea, too.

PROFESSOR ALAN K. CAMPBELL: There is a large group within the field of public administration that does not endorse this general administration idea. If anything, there is a movement away from this now, at least to the position that the person should know something about what he is administering. There are, of course, some fields of knowledge in public administration in which techniques of administration can be learned, but the first requisite is a knowledge of the enterprise you are going to administer. People who have been trained in our schools of administration have gone primarily to staff positions in budget, personnel, planning, and so on, rather than to top executive positions.

PROFESSOR WILLBERN: I was trying to say that there is a middle ground between a person who knows nothing but administration and a person who knows nothing but his specialty.

DR. THOMAS H. HAMILTON (Vice-President for Academic Affairs, Michigan State University): I have been concerned with this question for a long while. It seems to me the university administrator needs two kinds of qualities, one of which probably can be taught and the other of which cannot. He needs wisdom, which I think cannot be taught directly; and he needs to be a craftsman, and I think craftsmanship can. My only tentative conclusion is that the administrator ought to be selected for his capacity for wisdom and then asked to undergo the experience that would help him as a craftsman. Of craftsmanship I think there is a lot to be learned.

PROFESSOR McCONNELL: I doubt that you can teach very much about how to administer. I am less optimistic than most of my friends. I am told you can teach a good deal about the techniques of personnel management, for example, but when I see the personnel managers in operation I have some questions about it.

PROFESSOR RALPH N. CAMPBELL: I would suggest that one of the reasons for the failure of such personnel managers is that they lack a basic knowledge of the institution in which they are operating as personnel managers. I would be reluctant to populate the staffs of colleges and universities with people who have been prepared in training programs in personnel and other general techniques and have not come up through the line.

PROFESSOR WILLBERN: Nonetheless, there are problems that are known. People have been working on administrative problems in and out of higher education for a long time.

PROFESSOR McCONNELL: There is a fundamental failure in ad-

ministration in the way resources of expertness are used—or rather
are not used. Administrators cannot possess the information upon
which to make wise judgments in all things. It is not necessary that
the university administrator have the training to do everything that
needs to be done. On the staffs of these institutions are people who
do possess the needed information, and these people ought to be
used.

I remember one institution which was pressed with labor difficulties some years ago. The last person the administrator consulted was
the professor of industrial relations. Many times the administrators
of our institutions do not recognize the special competence of their
own staff in dealing with the problems that may arise. It seems to
me a part of good administration to use expertness where you find it.

I don't mean to sit here and argue against any effort to teach, or
to learn, the art of administration, but I do have a deep suspicion of
the notion that after one has been trained in general administration,
one can administer almost any kind of enterprise. We have had
enough of that approach in the field of professional education, it
seems to me.

Role of the Dean, Department Chairman—and President's Secretary

CHAIRMAN ELLIS: Through most of the day the discussion has
been on the president's office. I haven't heard anyone suggest that a
large part of the problem of the relations between faculty and administration may rest in the department chairman—including how he is
selected and whether or not he has tenure as chairman. There is a
wide difference of practice. My observation has been that this is as
important a key to this problem as any administrative post you have.

PROFESSOR PETRY: I would agree with that, Mr. Chairman. The
best and worst administration I have seen has been at the depart-
ment-head level.

CHAIRMAN ELLIS: I think the difficulties come partly from the fact
that some institutions have given permanent tenure to department
chairmen and have to let them live out their careers. In these cases,
department heads may develop little tyrannies.

PROFESSOR PETRY: I ought to say that the last five years of my
work was spent under the headship of a former graduate student of

mine, an excellent man. We gave him the job even though he was the youngest man in the department.

DR. TYLER: At the University of Chicago the chairmen are recommended by the faculty of the department, and it has been my observation that very often they recommend some younger man.

CHAIRMAN ELLIS: I think where that method is followed there is likely to be a very democratic situation within the department anyway. A person doesn't take the chairmanship in order to promote himself. He knows that things will be run the same way no matter who is chairman. I think that is a very desirable procedure.

PROFESSOR McCONNELL: Speaking of department heads, it shouldn't be necessary to get an administrative title in order to get a higher salary or status in the university. At a certain university where I was a staff member, there were a good many department chairmen whose salaries were lower than other members of the department. This is an extremely important policy to establish.

PRESIDENT WILSON: I think it has come to be more generally the case that the gap between the professorial and administrative salaries has been narrowed. In many institutions that I could refer to, a number of people are paid more than the president is. You can push this so far that the incentives are lost for able men to accept administrative jobs. We are going to run out of top talent if we don't do some things to make administrative posts more attractive.

Another difficulty with academic administrative jobs that involve tenure is that when a faculty man moves into a really responsible administrative position he is virtually marking time in his own field during his period of administrative service. If he goes back five or ten years later to teaching or research, he is forever afterward likely to be penalized in terms of prestige if not of his professional advantage. What is the solution to that problem?

PROFESSOR McCONNELL: I can testify on that, at least about being five to ten years behind. I think it is not an insurmountable problem. Five years might be a tolerable period of partial loss in one's field. If there are perquisites attached to administrative positions including salary differentials appropriate to the greater financial demands upon the administrative officer, but not greater basic remuneration, administrators would be more willing to resume their faculty positions.

DEAN BEACH: It seems to me that when we come to the matter of frictions, it is the dean, whether he is the dean of the graduate school or the dean of the college, who is the key figure in the alleviation of these frictions. The president, with all his other duties as fund-raiser and as possible educational philosopher and leader, is busy enough. The dean is the one who has to carry the burden, and if he is properly qualified by his background and experience, he can do it.

CHAIRMAN ELLIS: In many institutions, he would be the provost or the vice-president.

DEAN BEACH: Yes, it is the role or the function that I have in mind.

PROFESSOR WILLBERN: I hope we shall have time to discuss the nonacademic administrator and what his role is and ought to be. He is an essential part of the team. But his role is one that causes a lot of friction, and it may not be necessary.

DR. TYLER: A very important group is the female secretaries and other assistants who have been there long enough to run much of the communications system on the formal and informal levels. They exert a tremendous influence. I have known administrators who have been made or broken by the kind of persons they have had at the desk just outside their office.

Bringing Ideas from Outside the Campus to the Faculty

PRESIDENT SULLIVAN: How can information and ideas that come from research in education, from conferences, and so on outside the institution be communicated to faculties effectively? Suppose there is a lot of research of the kind Dr. Tyler discussed from which some light is shed on group behavior: how can the findings that a faculty should know about be conveyed to members of the faculty, many of whom are not interested in research of this kind? If the information comes through the administration of the college or university, it is heavily discounted if not mistrusted. The same kind of problem exists in getting one's faculty to consider educational policies or techniques that are applied in other institutions. Usually it is the administrators who talk about these things and who go back and try to explain them. There is all the distortion in communication that Ralph Tyler points out.

Dr. TYLER: One method by which this may be avoided is to attack a problem, not through the administration, but through a faculty task force which visits some of the places where things are going on that your faculty might want to consider. This is a fairly common method. I realize that some faculty members are skeptical about the intent or accuracy of the administrator's statements—sometimes for good reasons; but there is nothing to prevent direct communication going on among faculty members, and arrangements for direct exposure of members of the faculty to the ideas or experiences concerned may lead to this.

Advisability of Clear Definitions of Responsibility

PROFESSOR WILLBERN: In any big institution, to what degree is it necessary or desirable to put our policies and practices into written rules? I have been a little bothered by some of the suggestions that it is desirable to define roles as carefully as possible—to have manuals so that everybody will know exactly what is expected of him, what the criteria for promotion are, what the duties of a department are, and so on.

There are, of course, places where the policies need to be pinned down, but you can cause trouble by defining when you don't have to define and by trying to spell out things that are not ready yet to be spelled out and may never be. I don't know where the line is between the desirability of crystallizing and the desirability of leaving relationships fluid. In many cases relationships have to change with individuals. A set of rules for one dean may not fit his successor.

CHAIRMAN ELLIS: In general, you would say it would be better to go mighty slow on the rules. Don't adopt rules if you can help it?

PROFESSOR WILLBERN: I don't want to generalize. All I am saying is that it is not safe to take either extreme. Certainly you do need some crystallization sometimes, but too much of this can be a rigid, unpleasant yoke.

Dr. TYLER: Would you consider the bylaws of Cornell University, which Professor Ralph N. Campbell summarized, too rigid?

PROFESSOR WILLBERN: I had that impression a little.

PROFESSOR FUCHS: I guess this is where my professional approach is different. I believe in enactments where you can really say what you propose.

PROFESSOR WILLBERN: I recognize the advantage of them. I think there are some dangers as well.

PROFESSOR RALPH N. CAMPBELL: I was the one who brought up the question of criteria for promotion. Let me give a specific example in respect to promotion in adult education services. We have certain individuals in the extension operations of our school who have regular academic appointments. One of our personnel procedures provides that when an individual is promoted to tenure rank there is a discussion between the dean of the school and the faculty at that level or higher levels of whether the individual should be promoted. Inevitably, the question arises of what scholarly research and publication the individual has contributed. The fact is that a man who is devoting his full time to adult education activities, chiefly or entirely away from the campus, is not likely to do any scholarly research and publication. Yet he is always cast up against the criterion.

It seems to me that it is important for an individual coming into this kind of role either to understand that he will be required to do scholarly research (and it is necessary also that his duties and responsibilities be so established as to permit him to do it), or that it be an established policy that for these people scholarly research is not a criterion for promotion.

PROFESSOR McCONNELL: It seems to me that there are certain procedural matters in which formal enactments are quite desirable. My own experience in a case involving a faculty member who had refused to testify before a congressional investigating committee persuades me that it is well for the bylaws of the university to specify the procedure to be gone through in assessing the fitness of such an individual to remain on the faculty. Of course, this procedure may have to be changed from time to time, but having such a procedure established is a protection both for the faculty man and for the administration.

I have looked into some colleges recently where there was very real question of whether the faculty had the power to do any on the things mentioned in the Cornell bylaws that were summarized. We suggested that such points be made explicit to avoid the intrusion of boards of trustees in what should be prerogatives of the faculty.

I agree, though, that at times established rules are severe restrictions upon needed adjustment. I have never been very anxious, for example, to see the duties of deans spelled out except in the very broadest terms. A faculty will let one dean do things that it won't let another dean do—appropriately so, it seems to me.

PRESIDENT WHITAKER: You can get into trouble in defining the faculty area, too. Suppose the faculty at my institution were to decide that ROTC should be thrown out. That could very well be cutting over into the prerogatives of the board of trustees. Such a decision has something to do with the whole character of the institution.

PROFESSOR RALPH N. CAMPBELL: In determining the role of the institution—for example, in establishing new schools or programs— I think someone responsive to the general public interest has to be the determining body. Consultation with the faculty in making such decisions is essential but I believe responsibility for this kind of decision should not be turned over to the faculty, particularly because of the tendency for the perpetuation of our own kind. What kinds of universities would we have today if the faculties of the 1700's had themselves determined the role of the institution? We might still be concentrating on Latin and Greek and theology.

PROFESSOR McCONNELL: On the other hand, taking the principle that the trustees should deal only with broad general policy, I have tired to categorize which of a great variety of specific activities are appropriate for consideration and action by the board of trustees and which should be prerogatives of the faculty. I found that I had great difficulty in making a neat classification.

CHAIRMAN ELLIS: Deciding whether a given subject should start with the faculty and go to the board, start and stop with the faculty, or start with the board as an administrative proposition rather than with the faculty, gives the president some of his worst headaches. As an example, if you take something through the faculty and the board turns it down, you have a bad relationship that you might have avoided if you had put it directly to the board.

PROFESSOR RALPH N. CAMPBELL: There was a distinction in my thinking which I believe is pretty important. The responsibility of the faculty for educational policy is interwoven with budget-making and other administrative decisions. This creates a no man's land of authority and responsibility and makes specific definitions hazardous. But where the personal interest of the individual faculty mem-

ber is involved—questions of compensation, promotion, and so on—
I can see quite a difference in the degree to which specific criteria
need to be spelled out.

President Sullivan: This is extremely interesting to me, having
recently moved into a presidency and having to think through a
great many questions of policy and what to do with these questions.

I have certainly found that there is an enormous amount of flexibility in the procedures, no matter what has been said in writing.
Even if your board meets fairly frequently, the initiative of *what*
goes to the board and *when* it goes lies very largely with the president. It seems to me that only rarely would you want to have bylaws
or regulations, save for statements of fairly broad principle, which
would have the effect of removing this power of initiative, this
power of timing, from the president's hands. You cannot place the
power to do that in the hands of any committee.

Professor Ralph N. Campbell: In the bylaws which I spoke of
yesterday, different kinds of wording are used with regard to different functions. The provision says, for example, the *consideration* of
educational policy; it says the *determination* of some other things;
it says *recommends to the board* with regard to certain other things.

Professor Fuchs: Mr. Chairman, this seems to me to get to the
heart of our problem. As a member of a promotions committee I
have found a statement of criteria for promotion very helpful. Even
when in my opinion it was wrong in some particular, at least it
could be followed; and if it were wrong, it could be changed. It
helped to avoid arbitrariness or the charge of arbitrariness even
though it couldn't be sufficiently explicit to afford automatic guidance.

In respect to allocation of responsibility, it seems to me to be all-
important to make as clear as possible where responsibility rests. In
the matter of student discipline, for example, I ran across a situation
recently where there was a severe conflict between the president
and the faculty about whether there should be rather specific regulation of drinking on the campus. The faculty debated it back and
forth and finally voted contrary to the president's views. Well, he
was unhappy, quite naturally. He may have been right on the issue.
Now I understand the students are suddenly entering into the mat-

ter, and the student senate is going to consider whether to adopt some regulations.

It seems to me that is bad. It ought to be known from the setup of the institution where the responsibility for regulation on this matter rests; then the appropriate body should wrestle with it. The issue should not have to be passed around from one to the other as in this case.

PRESIDENT SULLIVAN: I agree that it is desirable to have some well-agreed-upon guide lines as to responsibility in general areas. At the same time I think you can err badly in making them too specific. Where procedures *are* spelled out, it seems to me important that there be full explanation by the administration to the faculty, both of the procedures themselves and of the setting in which they are to be used. When these matters are not understood, a lot of friction may occur.

CHAIRMAN ELLIS: We have a definite allocation to the faculty of matters of curriculum, student discipline, and other things. Any actions that affect those fields I never bother to refer to the board. Beyond this, there is no subject on which the faculty cannot make recommendations to the board, whether it is compensation policy, insurance, retirement plans, or anything of that kind. Anything that comes up outside the statutes goes to the board for approval. The board holds a sort of residual power in areas not specifically included in the rules, but they have given up their power over things like curriculum that are in the rules.

PROFESSOR RALPH N. CAMPBELL: The important point is that there be understanding of who is going to make given types of decisions in the event of conflict. It may rarely be necessary to resort to this authority, and when you do resort to it, doing so may indicate that cooperation has broken down. But if the "point of last resort" is not known and a decision needs to be made, the vacillation which results is much more frustrating than having someone go ahead and make the decision.

PROFESSOR WILLBERN: This is a problem in constitution-making. The most critical points you have to include in the basic "law." Matters of personnel procedure and tenure can be so full of tension that they need to be spelled out. But you can go much too far in other areas. I think an excellent analogy in this regard is provided by the Constitution of the United States, on the one hand, and the constitutions of many of our states, on the other, which go into great detail. The first is the one that lasts and lasts; it is vague at the proper places.

PROFESSOR MCCONNELL: There is another consideration—the distinction between the prerogatives of the board of trustees and those of the president of the institution. This matter will be determined in many cases by the relationship between the executive officer and the governing board. If you try to determine in too great detail what the prerogatives of the executive should be, you may find yourself more restricted than an executive whose prerogatives depend primarily on the confidence of his governing board. What an executive can do, and sometimes what a faculty can do, is determined by this relation of confidence between the bodies. If you try to govern these matters by exact bylaws, you may find yourself more, rather than less, restricted. Are these sound generalizations?

PRESIDENT ADERHOLD: There are special problems here in states which have a single board for a number of institutions. In these systems, difficulties may arise when the board changes a statute applying to all institutions because of an incident or problem that may exist at only one institution.

Techniques for Dealing with "Hot Issues" in a Faculty

PROFESSOR PETRY: Has anyone experimented with public hearings in a time of intense, campus-wide discussion of some particular issue? We are talking about ways to reduce tension, and the public hearing has sometimes proved useful.

On one occasion at Cornell, the faculty committee dealing with the problem of fraternity initiations sat for over a year on this question. Then it occurred to us that the matter was producing tension and that the report, when made, would increase the tension. We wanted to reduce the tension before the report was issued. We held full-dress public hearings that ran through three evenings—heard faculty, students, townspeople, alumni, and others. When the report came out, we hardly got coverage in the campus newspaper.

PROVOST FELS: We have at Columbia a faculty-student-administration group called the Committee on Student Organizations, in which we use the hearing technique. I think it is a good device. It can present difficulties, but every device presents difficulties, and we do find that it tends to quiet the tensions before they arise.

DEAN BEACH: Dr. Petry, is there any objection to having hearings before open faculty sessions?

PROFESSOR PETRY: In our case so many students were involved that we had to put the meetings in the evenings rather than at faculty meetings.

DEAN BEACH: We had this same problem up for consideration that you describe. We had a faculty meeting which lasted from four in the afternoon until ten o'clock at night without a break. Forty-five members of the faculty spoke; witnesses were present. We agreed before we sat down that we would settle the question, and we did settle it.

PROFESSOR PETRY: I think the hearing can have a very considerable effect on student and alumni opinion. But we should not spoil it by using it on small or inappropriate items.

PROVOST FELS: A related device used extensively at Columbia College is called the "faculty smoker." No important or controversial matter is brought directly to the faculty in a formal manner.

PROFESSOR PETRY: You caucus on it first?

PROVOST FELS: In an informal way and by an informal vote. The subject of discussion is presented at the smoker and there is a great deal of open discussion, with no vote. Only when the dean and the Committee on Instruction feel that the faculty is ready to vote do they convene the faculty for a formal meeting.

CHAIRMAN ELLIS: We often do that, too. We have informal meetings of divisional faculties, and at times the Faculty Club and the AAUP chapter call meetings and there is a lot of informal discussion. When you get your formal faculty meeting, everybody has had his say and the vote is taken without difficulty.

PROFESSOR WILLBERN: These are devices which recognize the social nature of the decision process. If as many people can be involved in the decision as is feasible under the circumstances, the decision, it seems to me, will be taken in a less tense atmosphere.

PROFESSOR MCCONNELL: This comment is anything but profound but perhaps it's a good one to close on. One of my associates, an administrator, was deeply hurt one time by some quite irresponsible faculty activities. I remember saying to him, "Did you think they weren't human beings?"

I think one cause of the difficulties we are discussing is that we tend to assume, in the case of either faculty members or administrators, that the characteristics of human nature are suspended. I think we would be much more effective in our relationships if we would assume that the motivations of people in education are essentially like the motivations of other people. This would lead us not to attribute a monopoly of ethical wisdom and virtue either to the administration or to the faculty.

Proposals for Further Study or Action

THE FOLLOWING SUGGESTIONS AND IDEAS FOR STUDY OR OTHER FORMS of action were advanced in the course of the work conference. For the most part these proposals were not discussed as to practicability, priority, or relationship to programs already under way. Some of the ideas may be practicable only on the level of the individual campus, others at some other level or at several levels. Undoubtedly some are not feasible under any design or auspices at the present time. The suggestions are set forth in this concluding section as a rough indication of the outcomes of the conference that pointed toward further action.

1. Encourage the study of the college or university as a social organization, including problems of administration, by collaborative research among scholars from the fields represented at this conference and others, such as anthropology, communications, and group dynamics.

2. Undertake case studies of university administrations in order to determine the structure of power and the loci of decision-making as a basis for analyzing the relation of actual decision-making practices to institutional objectives and to an "ideal" allocation of the various types of decisions that must be made.

3. Conduct research to establish the extensiveness, nature, and causes of conflicts between teaching and administrative staffs, including studies of the roles of various types or categories of persons (teachers, "researchers," presidents, business managers, public relations officers, student personnel officers, admissions officers, trustees, legislators, state financial officers, wealthy donors) in contributing to these tensions.

4. Study the department head as a mediating agent between teaching and administrative forces—the procedures by which department heads are appointed, length of term, emoluments, conduct of departmental affairs, reciprocal relations with the dean.

5. Identify and appraise the trends of the last few decades in the growth of university administrative organization, including major changes in procedures (such as in admissions and counseling)—the

facts of change, their causes, extent, and effects in relation to performance of academic functions and in relation to over-all objectives.

6. Study the practices, conditions, and needs of communication in the large university.

7. Study the types of top-level organization in respect to the distance that various forms of organization create between members of the faculty and top administration.

8. Appraise the role of financial, statistical, and other critical appraisal data in contributing to or in complicating internal communications.

9. Study the appropriate role of the college president as educational leader.

10. Identify and describe examples of "team administration."

11. On the premise that problems of faculty-administration relations can gain as much from discussion as from systematic research, encourage inclusion of some of these problems on the agenda of various local, state, regional, and national meetings.

12. Appraise the state of campus tension in relation to faculty and student productivity.

13. Prepare a descriptive report concerning college and university statutes and bylaws for faculty, board, and administrative officers, with a statement of principles to guide the development and maintenance of such statutes and bylaws. Contents might include (a) charters and bylaws; (b) statutes general to the college or university; (c) faculty "constitutions" and operating procedures; (d) budget procedures.

14. Catalog ways and means of involving large faculty groups with administration in productive discussion of goals and priorities.

15. With respect to the tensions among younger faculty members, study the assignments given to these teachers, their conditions of work, and the bearing of these conditions upon their satisfactions, performance, and aspirations.

16. Study the tensions which develop *within* faculties—for example between younger and senior ranks—and the procedures by which a faculty handles such issues.

17. Study the utility of the development of academic communities within large institutions, through the academic units, residential units, and other arrangements.

AMERICAN COUNCIL ON EDUCATION

Arthur S. Adams, *President*

The American Council on Education is a *council* of national educational associations; organizations having related interests; approved universities, colleges, teachers colleges, junior colleges, technological schools, and selected private secondary schools; state departments of education; city school systems and private school systems; selected educational departments of business and industrial companies; voluntary associations of higher education in the states; and large public libraries. It is a center of cooperation and coordination whose influence has been apparent in the shaping of American educational policies and formation of educational practices during the past forty years.